Books are keys
   to wisdom's treasure;
Books are paths
   that upward lead:
Books are gates
   to lands of pleasure,
Books are friends,
      Come, let us read

THIS BOOK BELONGS TO

JULIA W. MATTHEWS

# THE BEWITCHED PARSONAGE

A House divided against itself can't stand.

Better is a dry morsel and quietness therewith than a house full of sacrifices, and strife. Prov 17 ver 1

He loveth transgression that loveth strife; and he that exalteth his gait seeketh destruction. ver 19.

He that hath a froward heart findeth no good; and he that hath a perverse spirit falleth into mischeif ver 20

A reproof entereth more into the heart of a wise man more than an hundred stripes into a fool. ver 10.

He also that is slothful in his work is brother to him that is a great waster. Proverbs 18.9 ver.

The fear of the LORD tendeth to life; and he that hath it shall abide satisfied; he shall not be visited with evil. Prov 19 ver 23.

Charlotte Bronte finished this sampler April the 1 1828.

Reproduction of a sampler made by Charlotte Brontë. *Courtesy, The Bibliographical Society and Emery Walker.*

# The Bewitched Parsonage

The Story of THE BRONTËS

WILLIAM STANLEY
BRAITHWAITE

COWARD-MCCANN, INC. NEW YORK

To Edith

The Youngest Daughter

*Preface*

TO TELL again the story of the Brontës is to invite the captious eye of the literary historian. That cannot be avoided whatever the literary subject may be. The creative artist in literature is grist to every critic's mill. But critics have made appropriations which have excluded the interest of the general reader. This has been the case, and in a larger measure, I think, with the Brontës than with any other authors, whose lives and works have had such a long and familiar influence upon the reading public.

The tragic drama of the lives of the Brontë family has so colored and tempered the qualities and spirit of the Brontë novels that, in any appraisal of the writings, it is as difficult as it is undesirable to separate them. The fault is not in the eager willingness to interweave the realities of the Brontës' personal history with their creative and imaginative work, but with the injection, arbitrarily and conclusively, of critical ideas into the meaning and character of both the facts of personal history and the imaginative representations of the authors.

The general reader who has read the Brontë novels—and who hasn't?—seeking enlightenment about them and their authors, is more often than not confused by this welter of interpretations and explanations. He wants to know about them, but is discouraged from learning when confronted with the tangle of subtleties that must be unwound before reaching an understanding of the Brontë genius.

vii

The story herewith told of the Brontë genius has attempted to take a straight course. In its biographical and literary phases, it is hoped that both the information and interpretation has the quality and interest of a narrative.

The lives of the Brontë sisters are stories as intriguing as the stories that made their novels. With every one of the three it was a tragic story. The novels reflected this tragedy. That is why, I think, it has been important to treat the novels with the fullness that has been attempted here. If they overbalance the straight biographical material, they may well serve to extend the revelations that the private lives of the sisters in the Haworth Parsonage yielded with such reluctance. When we stop to consider that essentially all the facts of their lives that have any validity are contained in Charlotte's voluminous correspondence, the novels are as important biographically as they are artistically. And Charlotte was not above tempering her letters with her imaginative emotions while recording the domestic life of the family.

The story of the Brontës reiterates one overwhelming truth, and this is that life is an enigma. With some individuals it is easily solved and forgotten. With the four Brontë children it leaves us bewildered—as it has for a century—and only sure of the emotions that fired them and the spirit that winged them.

W. S. B.

*New York, 1950*

viii

# Contents

# CONTENTS

# Illustrations

# THE BEWITCHED PARSONAGE

*Chapter* 1   FUROR SCRIBENDI

THE creative force in man is a fugitive one. It rises from some mysterious origin and finds sanctuary in the blood and brain of certain individuals. In the early Greek civilization the creative faculty was thought to be a gift of the gods, a fire that set the imagination aflame, enraged the emotions. It was born of religious faith, and was redeemed in tragedy. The poet, sculptor, dramatist of Greece practiced his art as an appeasement of the gods, and was in turn touched and transfigured in the light of inspiration. Since neither psychology nor aesthetics was known, as we know them today, there was no attempt to probe man's conscious or subconscious, to plumb the depths of his symbolism. Aristotle was a very wise man, but even Aristotle left this *rage,* this process of creation, to the gods. He certainly would not have attempted to explain the strange phenomenon of the Brontës, where the lightning struck many times in the same family! Not that we can explain it today, with modern methods of scientific investigation at our disposal, and with psychiatry itself by way of becoming an exact science.

For Freudian analysis has thus far failed to clarify the enigma. Nor does the *Mecanisme Cerebrale* of M. Nicolas Kostyleff, that genius can be measured by a mathematical yardstick, help us in the least. John Livingston Lowes, in his remarkable study of Coleridge's "Kubla Khan," tries bravely

3

to capture the elusive answer to what it is that birthmarks some men with genius, and by-passes most of us. He goes a long way toward solving the riddle. And the poet, William Blake, has interpreted it as the difference between the average man and the man endowed with the most intense sensibilities. But this, too, hardly seems to be the complete answer. Many an "average" man is possessed of acute sensibility, or susceptibility, yet cannot express it through the medium of art. In other words, he has not been star-crossed by that fever of the blood which heightens imagery to the point where it communicates reality by fusing it with insight to make a symbol which is itself another reality. There are psychological factors here which, for all the advances in the practice of science, are still fundamentally unexplained. Heredity, experience, environment, all play a role—their proportions being difficult to gauge, due in great part to the quantitative and qualitative variations in the individuals concerned. While one tries to detect the pattern, it falls away in one's hands, dissolves as one concentrates upon it, like a mist in the sun's rays.

But most mysterious of all are the instances in which an entire family is stricken with genius, a family that seems to have drunk at the same Pierian spring. There is no more extraordinary example of such a family in all literature than that of the Brontës, who lived in the Haworth Parsonage, on the West Riding of England's Yorkshire, during the early nineteenth century. The parents, Patrick Brontë and Maria Branwell, the one from Ireland, the other from Cornwall, were ordinary people, but within them lay sparks that were to be touched off by the union to give us an explosion, so to speak, of *furor scribendi* in their progeny.

By inheritance, tradition, and childhood experience, the

father had traveled down Ireland's folkways. He came from the soil; he understood the uninhibited physical appetities of the peasant; he was imbued with the spirit of the supernatural; he knew the tragedy of poverty that is so often akin to comedy, comedy that is close to tragedy. Although he rose above his environment and attended one of England's great universities, earning a bachelor's degree in the humanities, his primitive instincts never bowed entirely before the discipline and moderation of men of birth. He remained illiterate in his marital relations, his belief in the unquestioned authority of the male of the species. Even when he became a vicar in the Anglican Church, his adopted faith, his intellectual and emotional attitudes had undergone little change. No faith, of whatever kind, appears to have softened his crude ambitious nature. He was impervious to the physical (and spiritual) needs of his wife and children. What had sufficed for his own meager existence as a child could suffice for them. He seems to have nourished, even with a kind of pride, a scorn of refined living, of all beauty manifest in color or texture or workmanship. What was good enough for him, he implied, was good enough for his children. Such a philosophy, if one can dignify it by such a name, could only make a stark and desolate atmosphere, in the home or in the heart, for the woman who bore him six children in seven years and died of cancer before the youngest could call her by the name of mother. And it naturally raised a heavy inscrutable barrier between him and the four little ones who were to make his name immortal.

Maria Branwell, on the other hand, was born of a respectable middle-class family in Penzance, Cornwall. The family apparently had pride and tradition, and some substance. If their manners perhaps showed a slight hauteur, as

5

in the person of "Aunt Elizabeth," Maria's sister, it was because the Branwells were accustomed to a position in society. The Brontës had no position in Ireland. And, even though Patrick was a university graduate when he wooed and won Maria, her family undoubtedly felt that he was not her equal. As the years passed and they saw her the victim of a ruthless helpmate, an unrestrained marriage bed, and dire poverty, they must have said, in thought if not in words, that it was only to be expected. But even the opportunity to upbraid Maria for her foolhardy love, her loyalty and devotion to a man who gave so little in return, was short-lived. Eight years of marriage and Maria Branwell Brontë was buried in the little Haworth Church, where her two eldest daughters, Elizabeth and Maria, were soon to join her. Indeed, Patrick Brontë was to outlive not only his wife but all his children.

The characters of both parents were deeply affected by their religious upbringing. Maria Branwell was born and raised a Methodist, Patrick Brontë a Presbyterian, yet both were united in the Episcopal Church. However, religion dealt variously with the temperaments of Patrick and Maria. Whereas it made her a woman of strong conscience, God-fearing and humble, simple and sincere and uncomplaining, in him it produced a hard core of religious zeal and moral judgment. He carried out the *laws* of the Church to the final letter. God ordained that man should marry: he had married. God ordained that man should create from the seed of his loins: this he had done in full measure. What more was necessary? It was not required that he sit at his wife's deathbed, or visit his daughter Anne when she also lay dying in Scarborough by the Sea, or give his daughter Charlotte away in marriage.

6

Charlotte and Emily Brontë have both given us a somewhat harsh opinion of an unnatural father, often directly, more often under various disguises, as in the first chapters of Emily's *Wuthering Heights*. A poem of Emily's describes him as

bland and kind,
But hard as hardest flint the soul that lurks behind,

and she tells us he was a man who "took for granted Original Sin and his own supreme authority," that he was a "hard, just judge," just according to the code she knows, unjust according to the code she feels. Edith Ellsworth Kinsley sums him up as "a good man, but cold, hard and ambitious. His nature had a deep and sunless source. . . . If he was displeased, no happy reconciliation could be had with him—no ruth met ruth. . . . It is reputed that he never spoke an unkind word to his wife, but he did not speak many. He was patient; he prided himself on Christian forbearance; he remarked that he was not in the habit of cherishing vexation; but his eye was a cold blue hem, and he spoke in a tone that mortified pride." Roamer Wilson adds, "Emily's portrait [of her father] is perfectly fair." This, then, was the sort of man the gentle Maria had chosen for her husband. It was soon obvious to both that they were peculiarly unsuited to each other, and each turned to his appointed task: Patrick to his study and his vocation, Maria to her childbearing and to the management of a growing family in a home darkened by illness and privation.

It is of course probable that Patrick Brontë's nature suffered a sea change as he saw his own hopes and ambition gradually reduced to naught by the exigencies of living. He himself had fostered literary aspirations, and undoubtedly the overcrowded household, the disturbance of the children,

7

interfered with his writing. Anyway, his literary pursuits seemed to come to an abrupt close in 1818 when he published his fourth and last book, *The Maid of Killarney*. How much did the four children, born in the cramped rooms behind the grocery store in Thornton, who were to startle the world with their own literary genius, owe to the ambitious Irish peasant with his frustrated desires, and his inheritance of strong natural instincts battened down by overwhelming odds in a land foreign to his soul? And how much again to the quiet-hearted mother who also dreamed of other scenes than these, scenes shifting against a curtain of wild sea foam on the Cornish coast? Something of both, of course, went into the forging of the destinies of these children. From the farthest reaches of incompatibility and disparity a man and a woman crossed paths, and where they crossed the elements of their natures fused to a white-hot flame of creative power, not only once but again and again.

A like power was discernible in every one of the six children. Even Maria and Elizabeth showed signs of possessing it, before they fell victim to the dread disease that carried them away in childhood, and eventually claimed Emily and Anne. These two little girls were the first sacrifices to the insensibility of the parent to the malnutrition and physical hardship, the damp, dark house and unsanitary conditions, that continuously endangered the health of the entire family. Their mode of living shattered the frail immaturity of all the children. It would seem that spirit alone was what kept some of them alive to fulfill their appointed destinies: Anne to write *Agnes Grey* and *The Tenant of Wildfell Hall*, Charlotte *Jane Eyre* and *Villette*, and Emily the crowning achievement, *Wuthering Heights*.

Thus, to repeat, we have in the Brontë sisters a case of multiple genius that fits no known category of interpretation. There were obviously biologic forces unleashed that have no adequate explanation, either in medicine or in psychiatry. It is possible that the reason so little attempt has been made to discover the roots of the Brontë phenomenon is that biographers are fearful lest they should be found to lie in the science of pathology. There are clearly disturbing symptoms in the "behavior patterns" of any one of the Brontë children one cares to name. An exploration into their creative faculties is no mere simple analysis of cause and effect. It must entail a descent into the realm of the subconscious where, in some mystical way, the creative impulses of four members of the same family were united in a Gordian knot. And we must needs take under observation the strange way in which the cords of inspiration were cut at the point where any one of them was crossed directly by the world at large. It was as if the currents that flowed into creative channels, illuminating the inner mind and spirit, blacked out as surely as if a switch had been thrown, when other faces, other places intervened.

As children, the three sisters and the brother played at writing with all the seriousness of adults, and with a strange secrecy. They poured into their compositions a mental and emotional energy out of all proportion to their scanty physical stamina. Even more amazing than the drive itself were the character and passion, the naïve sophistication, of the tales and romances they created. The histories of the Angrian and Gondal Empires are tumultuous chronicles of love and revolution, diplomacy and conquest, cruelty and sacrifice. They are dream fabrications fashioned to make possible an acceptance of the misery and loneliness of reality. Yet into these

9

tales is woven a web of thought, a mature conception that seems primal in its origins, and which can almost be translated into a philosophy. The social and psychological implications of Charlotte's *Jane Eyre* or *Shirley*, of Emily's *Wuthering Heights*, or of Anne's *The Tenant of Wildfell Hall* have their seed in the Angrian and Gondal child's play. Angria and Gondal were outlets for forces that could not be contained. Although these epics were born of childhood they cannot be said to be juvenilia. They seem to explode from an inner compulsion, atavistic in nature, whose chemistry is obscurely buried in time. The Brontë children did not live the normal life of childhood and youth. The brief periods they were away from home, at Cowan Bridge School, or Roe Head, or the Heger Pensionnat in Brussels, or as governesses in the homes of Yorkshire families, served only to heighten their desire to return to the nest on the moors. Indeed they were alien to any other environment than that of the West Riding. They were attached, as by an umbilical cord, to the earth, to something primeval in nature, and to each other.

*Furor scribendi!* It is what possessed Emily, Charlotte, Anne, and Branwell Brontë. It is self-explanatory and yet explains nothing. It is a name for a seething brew of spiritual and emotional daring and desire. The desire to write came as a spontaneous overflow of the imagination—an extraordinary awareness of light and color, space and motion, love and hate. The intensity of concentration needed to transfer the imagery to paper is another miracle beyond our comprehension. It could only have come from that "crepuscular twilight" where Henry James traces the subtle motivations of character for which he is famous. But though James located this dim region where lie the springs of our beings, he was still unable to explain the source beyond the source, the source below all sources, from which the Brontë children received their strength. The wine of creation boiled up from subterranean depths we know not of, or what or where or when, and could not be stayed short of death. There was no respite till genius had run its tide.

*Chapter* II   THE BRUNTYS OF AHADERG

Patrick Brontë, the father of the Brontë children, was born in the Parish of Ahaderg, County Down, in Northern Ireland, on March 17, 1777. Since March 17 is the day of Ireland's patron saint, Saint Patrick, he was naturally named in the saint's honor.

The family name has been variously known as Prunty, Brunty, and Brontë. Hugh Prunty, Patrick's father, probably changed the name to Brontë, although it has been suggested that Patrick made the change when he registered at St. John's College, Cambridge.

Hugh Prunty (or Brontë) had ten children, Patrick being the eldest. They were one and all remarkable for their beauty and strength, the girls being as Amazonian as their brothers were Herculean. The stock was Irish peasant, going back many generations in the region north of the river Boyne. The story of the family, followed to its dim sources, is filled with tales of character and romance. Augustine Birrell, in his study of Charlotte, published in 1887, remarked that "nobody has even been at pains to discover anything about Charlotte Brontë's nine uncles and aunts." Six years later, in 1893, William Wright published *The Brontës in Ireland, or Facts Stranger Than Fiction.* Here, for the first time, was something about Charlotte's forebears, her father and mother, as well as her uncles "and her cousins and her aunts." And, although

Dr. Wright's book aroused considerable controversy, many of his facts proving to *be* fiction, he is the only biographer who has taken the trouble to trace the Brontë ancestry in Ireland. All other biographers, including Mrs. Gaskell, have given their attention to the Brontës in England. Dr. Wright relates, with partisan enthusiasm it must be admitted, the history of the Irish Pruntys through the two generations preceding Emily's, and there is an atmosphere of extravagance and wildness in his memoir which is strongly articulated in her *Wuthering Heights*. In other words, the children of Patrick Brontë and Maria Branwell must have been told many tales, remembered and half-remembered, of their Irish heritage.

For instance, the story of Heathcliff, in *Wuthering Heights*, comes straight from the Prunty household in Ahaderg. Prunty's father, the great-grandfather of Emily and Charlotte, was a prosperous farmer and cattle raiser who sold his stock in the Liverpool markets. Returning from one of his journeys he brought with him a waif, a foundling child, whom he proceeded to make a member of the family. Because of the boy's swarthy complexion it was believed he might have been born in Wales, and he was given the name of Welsh. Like Heathcliff, Welsh, when he came of age, acquired the property of his benefactor, and his foster-brother, Hugh, became his ward. And although Welsh promised to make Hugh his heir, and give him the education that was his due, he sent him away from his home in Drogheda to live with an uncle in Ahaderg, where he grew up in misery. The bitterness and resentment Hugh Prunty must have felt as a result of such injustice undoubtedly affected his character adversely in some ways, but it may also have been responsible for making him a man of strong will and ambitious dreams. And in addition he was endowed with a striking personality and delightful imagination.

Although the family was Protestant for generations, Hugh Prunty married a Catholic. Alice McClory was the "prettiest girl in the county," and Hugh did not let her religion stand in the way of his desire to make her his wife. Her family is said to have objected strenuously, and the story is that the two young people were "the chief figures in a fierce religious drama." They met secretly at a spot known as the Courting Bower until betrayed by a servant, whereupon they eloped and were secretly married.

Alice McClory was not only a pretty girl but a very intelligent one, and she passed on her beauty and intelligence to her nine sons and daughters. Their first four children were boys, Patrick, William, Hugh, and James, and the following five were girls, Jane, Mary, Rose, Sarah, and Alice.

Dr. Wright vividly describes the daughters: "the Brontë girls were tall, red-cheeked, fair-haired, with dark eyelashes, and very handsome. They were massive strong-minded women; and, as they despised men in their own rank of life, only one of them married." His book also contains a sketch, written by his friend, Mr. McCracken, who had known the Pruntys: "I have seen all the sisters of Patrick Brontë except the one that was married. They were fine, stalwart, good-looking women, with rather a masculine build and carriage. They were not ordinary women. They were essentially women of character, and I think men were perhaps a little afraid of them."

The brothers, too, have been described, with typical Irish hyperbole, by a neighbor: "I remember seeing them as they marched in step across the field. Their style of marching and their whole appearance arrested our attention. They were

14

dressed alike in homespun and home-knitted garments that fitted them closely, and showed off to perfection their large, lithe, and muscular forms. They were all tall men, but with their close-fitting apparel and erect bearing they appeared to be men of gigantic stature. They bounded lightly over all the fences that stood in their way, all springing from the ground and alighting together; and they continued to march in step without apparent effort until they reached the public road, and then began in a businesslike way to settle conditions in preparation for a serious contest.... We had never seen men like the Irish Brontës, and we had never heard language like theirs. The quaint conceptions, glowing thoughts, and ferocious epithets, that struggled for utterance at their unlettered lips, revealed the original quarry from which the vicar's daughters chiselled the stones for their artistic castle-building, and closed the original fountain from which they drew their pathos and passion. Similar fierce originality and power are felt to be present in everything produced by the English Brontës; but in their case the intensity of energy is held in check by the Branwell temperament, and kept under restraint by education and culture." The physical attractions of these young men were generously bestowed on Branwell, Patrick's only son. Branwell also inherited other, less fortunate, family characteristics. He was given to the outbursts of hysteria, wild eloquence, pagan revelry, that were so much a part of the Prunty nature.

It naturally would follow that this Irish ancestry, colorful and exciting as it was, would have a strong influence on the imagination and writing of Hugh's grandchildren in England, who never saw him. It undoubtedly had an effect on their literary genius. Emily particularly seems to have drawn on this source for much of her material and many of her characters. Hugh Prunty's tales of his boyhood and youth, of his relations with the dark-complexioned Welsh, of the upheaval that took place in his life when he was transplanted to Ahaderg, of the countless superstitions passed from generation to generation, all these came down to the Brontë children in the English parsonage through their father's retelling. He must have told them of the wars, too, of the Battle of the Boyne, and the Battle of Ballynahinch, where his brother had fought. The Bruntys (or Pruntys) were Orangemen of Ulster, Protestants, believing in a free Ireland. Violence, then, and passionate protest, were in the Brontë blood.

According to Dr. Wright's record, one figure in particular was the villain of the piece. This was Gallagher, an old servant and retainer of the family, who came to give his entire allegiance to Welsh as Welsh gradually usurped the family estate. It was on Gallagher, more than on Welsh, that Hugh Prunty poured, as Dr. Wright says, "the copious vials of the Brontë satire, scorn and hatred." Gallagher becomes a vicious figure of talebearing, religious hypocrisy, and unctuous service to his master. Gallagher is recreated as Joseph in *Wuthering Heights*. Without a knowledge of Gallagher, it would be puzzling to know where Emily, secluded and inexperienced as she was, could have conceived the idea of the substance and temper of Joseph's character.

When Patrick Brontë left Ireland for Cambridge he never returned to his native land. But he carried with him a fund of tradition and story, handed down to him by a father who possessed, "like the bards of old," a power of illuminating the past. And he succeeded in impressing it upon his own children, so that the English moors of Haworth and the Irish fells of Ahaderg became inextricably woven into the fiction and poetry of Emily, Charlotte, and Anne.

*Chapter* III  PATRICK BRUNTY
INTO PATRICK BRONTË

As we have said, the nature and character of Patrick Brontë, whatever it may have become later as father and husband, was indelibly underscored by the peasant life from which he sprang. Yet his mind, unlike the minds of his young brothers and sisters, must have been filled with rebellious thoughts, with a desire to escape a provincial life bounded by farming and by trade. As the family gathered during the long autumn evenings around the furnace in the cabin kitchen, where the oats were roasted for the community, Patrick listened to his father's tales of derring-do, of the giants of Irish history, of the deeds of the Pruntys in the great wars, and wondered why he shouldn't be a warrior of a different kind. Something whispered that knowledge, the knowledge obtained from books, could be an open sesame to another world. Even this way would be hard and long, since there was no money to send him to school. But he would earn the money himself. He apparently made up his mind about it very young, and he never changed his course. It meant that the farm boy, whose horizons had for generations been bounded by the river Boyne and the Mourne Mountains, was destined to attend one of the two greatest English universities. He was to become a minister in the English Church. His rooms would be lined with the books he knew and loved.

17

Three of his four children would make original and permanent marks on English literature.

To earn the money necessary to buy the learning he needed, he went to work as a handloom weaver. By the time he was sixteen he had become very skillful, and not only was producing enough cloth for use at home but was selling it elsewhere. And when the production of flax was first introduced in Ulster he turned to the weaving of linens, and found an excellent market in the towns nearby, Banbridge and Newry. He carried his wares as far afield as Belfast in order to haunt the larger bookstalls, and to meet others who read books and talked about them.

At last an incident occurred that was definitely the turning point in Patrick's life. He was lying on the grass one afternoon in Emdale Fort, reading aloud to the sky from Milton's *Paradise Lost,* when the Reverend Andrew Harshaw, the village minister and schoolteacher, came by. Harshaw was so impressed by the boy's obvious love of poetry, by his finding and reading Milton, that he sat down with him then and there and suggested that Patrick do some supervised studying at the parsonage. "During those first years of study," Dr. Wright says, "young Brontë never allowed himself more than four or five hours of sleep at night. He used to sit in his Uncle Paddy's chimney corner reading Ovid and Virgil and Homer and Herodotus, and working out the problems of Euclid on the hearthstone with the blackened ends of his half-burnt splits." Before dawn Patrick would visit Mr. Harshaw in his bedroom at the rectory; from there he went to his loom for a twelve-hour work day.

As soon as Mr. Harshaw considered Patrick's studies sufficiently advanced he secured him a teaching position in the Glascar Hill Presbyterian Church School. There was a great

The Rev. P. Brontë. *Photograph by Walter Scott. Copyright, The Brontë Society.*

The Brontë Sisters by P. B. Brontë. *Copyright, National Portrait Gallery, London.*

deal of opposition to the appointment on the part of Presbyterian parents, Patrick's mother being Catholic. But Mr. Harshaw took matters firmly in hand and Patrick was given the job.

He remained at the Glascar School for some time and was very successful with the children, who came from the homes of farmers and tradespeople. Dr. Wright reports that "several little country boys who began their studies under Brontë succeeded in forcing their way to the universities; and some of them became professional men of eminence." In the meantime, Patrick continued his own education with Mr. Harshaw; and it was during the same period that he began to write poetry, intending to give the children pleasure, and inspire them to a love of writing as well as reading. Most of the poems appearing in *Cottage Poems,* published in 1811, were written then.

But all was not smooth sailing for Patrick at the Glascar School. An unfortunate and unnecessary entanglement with a young girl, one of his pupils, was responsible for the loss of his position there. The girl was the daughter of the most substantial farmer in the neighborhood. She was red-haired and attractive. One of her brothers caught Patrick kissing her and reported it at home. "War was instantly declared against the 'mongrel' and 'papish brat' who had dared to insult their daughter." They produced the love poems Patrick had been writing Helen as evidence of her consent to his advances. Helen, in the meantime, took his side against her family, which only helped to fan the flames of battle. Everyone concerned in the matter seems to have made himself somewhat ridiculous, but it was Patrick Brontë who stood to lose the most. Helen's father, being an influential pillar of the Glascar church, was able to pursuade the new minister to dismiss the young teacher. This was serious enough, but the effect of Patrick's folly went even further, for it weakened the friendship and devotion of Mr. Harshaw, who was severe in his censure. Yet Mr. Harshaw's interest in Patrick and his admiration for the boy's intellectual curiosity were so great that he eventually helped him obtain another position in the parish school at Drumballyroney. At the same time, realizing that Patrick was not likely to reach the goal they had both set for him—a university education—through his own Presbyterian connections, particularly after the Glascar episode, Mr. Harshaw recommended that Patrick enter the Episcopal Church. This was extraordinary advice, considering the time and the place, and indicates an amazingly broad viewpoint, a most generous nature, on the part of the Reverend Andrew Harshaw.

The Reverend Thomas Tighe, Episcopal vicar of the united parishes of Drumballyroney and Drumgooland, found Mr. Harshaw's protégé "an enthusiastic and excellent teacher." He was so appreciative of the young man's exceptional ability that he trusted him with the tutoring of his own children, and he himself continued giving Patrick the instruction he still needed for entering the university. So a great deal of credit is also due the Reverend Tighe, though of course not in the same degree as Mr. Harshaw, for discovering and forwarding Patrick Brontë's talents and ambition. The inner drive that makes some of us rise above our conditions, our environment, is as much a mystery as any other genius we may possess. Patrick Brontë had it in full measure. And although Mr. Harshaw and Mr. Tighe were intelligent enough to spot it, and generous enough to cultivate it, yet Patrick would have gone where he was going by one means or another. However, it is a great pity that there are no records of the conversations, exchange of ideas, that must have taken place between Patrick and his two mentors. They would be interesting from every standpoint, and might be very illuminating in explaining the philosophy and attitude of the man Patrick became. For, after he settled down at Haworth as vicar, the source of those qualities which lent enchantment to his nature, force to his dreams, seemed to wither away. When life bore down on him with relentless tragedies he could summon no inner strength to temper them with the gentleness of acceptance, the sweetness of endurance. Then he seemed to shrink from all human warmth and sympathy, and retreat into the lonely solace of his faith, which only succeeded in making him a colder and more forbidding man. There is nothing to indicate such a retreat from life in the accounts, which are very full and delightful, of his activities between his coming down from Cambridge and his marriage to Maria Branwell. During this period of gaiety and hope he seemed well on his way to fulfilling the promise that inspired Mr. Harshaw and Mr. Tighe to believe in his future, and stirred their hearts to give him help and courage. However, in his earlier relations with Mr. Harshaw and Mr. Tighe, there may have been indications of certain dark wells in his nature that drew their waters from the difficulties and sadness, perhaps largely unconscious at the time, of leaving his home and his family, and the fields and streams of his native land. It is quite possible that such a finality could demand a heavy price in later years.

*Chapter* IV    IRISH YOUTH
            AND CORNISH MAID

PATRICK BRONTË received his degree of
bachelor of arts at St. John's, Cambridge, in the spring of 1806.
He must have been duly proud. But Mr. Harshaw and Mr.
Tighe were undoubtedly just as proud, since their protégé
had now justified the faith and encouragement, the many
moments of anxiety, the long hours of toil, that Patrick's ad-
vancement had meant to them. For at St. John's the boy had
immediately won honors, and had continued to pay his entire
tuition and residence with scholarships and fellowships
throughout his years at the university. Four months after his
arrival he obtained one of the Hare Exhibitions, established
by Sir Ralph Hare, for "thirty of the poorest and best disposed scholars." Less than a year later he was granted one of
the Duchess of Suffolk's Exhibitions, also established for
students of poor circumstances, and both these awards were
continued through 1806 and 1807. In 1805 he won the Good-
man Exhibition. Over and above these sums from the grants,
he earned his spending money tutoring his fellow students.

There is a complete dearth of material of any kind regarding Patrick Brontë's years at Cambridge. Perhaps the only
detail we have concerning his college life is extracurricular:
since Napoleon was threatening invasion, the undergraduates
had formed a volunteer training corps, and Patrick found
himself drilling in company with Henry John Temple ( Lord

Palmerston-to-be) and the young Duke of Devonshire. But there is no record that Patrick formed any close friendships among his classmates, either then or later.

In October of 1806, a few months after taking his degree, Patrick Brontë entered Holy Orders. He was ordained in the Episcopal Church, and straightway became curate in the village of Weathersfield in a remote section of Essex County. During his three years in Weathersfield it is apparent that he was often involved in episodes similar to the unfortunate incident that ended his career at the Glascar School. There was not only Mary Bruder, whom he met in the home of her aunt, Miss Mildred Davey, where he boarded during the first months, but, as Mr. Clement Shorter remarks, "gossip had much to say concerning the flirtations of its Irish curate," both in Weathersfield and later in Dewsbury. Patrick seems to have actually fled before his reputation, from one curacy to the other, and, in 1811, he escaped from Dewsbury to Hartshead, on the West Riding of Yorkshire. It was indeed becoming high time that young Mr. Brontë should meet a young lady who would return his sentiments in kind and marry him forthwith, interference by fathers, uncles, brothers to the contrary. And, fortunately, the right opportunity suddenly materialized, in the summer of 1812, in the person of Maria Branwell. The courtship was whirlwind, leading to marriage by the consent of all concerned, even an uncle!

Maria Branwell had come to Yorkshire from Penzance, Cornwall, to visit her uncle, the Reverend John Fennel. She was an orphan, but her father had been a well-to-do merchant, the family well descended and thoroughly respected in Penzance. Mrs. Gaskell describes Maria Branwell as "extremely small in person; not pretty, but very elegant, and always dressed with a quiet simplicity of taste, which accorded well with her general character.... Mr. Brontë was soon captivated by the little, gentle creature, and declared that this time it was for life!" And this time Patrick's love did prosper, at least until he had attained his heart's desire. Everything conspired to forward the association and rapidly deepening affection of the lovers. Their engagement was thoroughly approved and blessed by Mr. Fennel, who joined his niece in writing her sisters in Penzance, announcing the betrothal and praising Mr. Brontë without reserve. There were picnics and parties and meetings on the moors—and love letters.

But it is when we come to the love letters that the first shadow seems to fall across this bright and hopeful romance. For although it is abundantly clear that there was a considerable correspondence between Patrick and Maria during the courtship, borne witness to by Maria's own letters and her many references to his, there is not a single letter of Patrick Brontë's to be found. During the four months of association before the marriage Maria wrote nine letters which we have intact. Mr. Brontë seems to have preserved these with considerable care, and many years later he gave them to Charlotte. Since he was sufficiently interested to make such an effort, why did neither Patrick nor Maria treasure the letters he wrote her? Did Mr. Brontë deliberately destroy them? Or did she? Or were they merely mislaid?

The nine letters Maria Branwell wrote between August 26 and December 5 clearly indicate that they were in answer to letters received. She was not the first to write, an etiquette quite in accord with her character and up-bringing. "My dear Friend," she opens her first letter, "This address is sufficient to convince you that I not only permit, but approve of yours to me—I do consider you as my friend." In her second,

24

dated September 5, "My dear Friend" has become "My dearest Friend," and she continues, "I have just received your affectionate and very welcome letter, and though I shall not be able to send this until Monday, yet I cannot deny myself the pleasure of writing a few lines this evening, no longer considering it a task, but a pleasure, next to that of reading yours." The third, September 11, begins, "Having spent the day yesterday at Miry Shay, a place near Bradford, I had not got your letter till my return in the evening, and consequently have only a short time this morning to write if I send it by this post. You surely do not think you *trouble* me by writing?"

However, the last two letters before her marriage do strike the first faint notes of warning that all is not well for the future; although the first of these, which I quote in full, is an expression of spirit and feeling prophetic of the woman who would one day be the mother of Emily Brontë.

My dear Saucy Pat,—Now don't you think you deserve this epithet far more than I do that which you have given me? I really know not what to make of the beginning of your last, the winds, and rocks almost stunned me. I thought you were giving me the account of some terrible dream, or that you had had a presentment of the fate of my poor box, having no idea that your lively imagination could make so much of the slight reproof conveyed in my last. What will you say when you get a *real, downright scolding?* Since you show such a readiness to atone for your offenses after receiving a mild rebuke, I am inclined to hope you will seldom deserve a severe one. I accept with pleasure your atonement, and send you a free and full forgiveness. But I cannot allow that your affection is more deeply rooted than mine. However, we will dispute no more about this, but rather embrace every opportunity to prove its sincerity and strength by acting in every

25

respect as friends and fellow-pilgrims travelling the same road, actuated by the same motives, and having in view the same end. I think if our lives are spared twenty years hence I shall then pray for you with the same, if not greater, fervour and delight that I do now. I am pleased that you are so fully convinced of my candour, for to know that you suspected me of a deficiency in this virtue would grieve and mortify me beyond expression. I do not derive any merit from the possession of it, for in me it is constitutional. Yet I think where it is possessed it will rarely exist alone, and when it is wanted there is reason to doubt the existence of almost every other virtue. As to the other qualities which your partiality attributes to me, although I rejoice to know that I stand so high in your good opinion, yet I blush to think in how small a degree I possess them. But it shall be the pleasing study of my future life to gain such an increase of grace and wisdom as shall enable me to act up to your highest expectations and prove to you a helpmeet. I firmly believe the Almighty has set us apart for each other; may we, by earnest, frequent prayer, and every possible exertion, endeavour to fulfil His will in all things! I do not, cannot, doubt your love, and here I freely declare I love you above all the world besides. I feel very, very grateful to the great Author of all our mercies for His unspeakable love and condescension towards us, and desire "to show forth my gratitude not only with my lips, but with my life and conversation." I indulge a hope that our mutual prayers will be answered, and that our intimacy will tend much to promote our temporal and eternal interest.

I suppose you never expected to be much the richer for me, but I am sorry to inform you that I am still poorer than I thought myself. I mentioned having sent for my books, clothes, etc. On Saturday evening about the time you were writing the description of our imaginary shipwreck, I was reading and feeling the effects of a real one, having then received a letter from my sister giving me an account of the vessel in which she had sent my box being stranded on the coast of Devonshire, in consequence of which the box was dashed to pieces with the violence of the sea, and all my little property, with the exception of a very few articles, swallowed up in the mighty deep. If this should prove the prelude to something worse, I shall think little of it, as it is the first disastrous circumstance which has occurred since I left home, and having been so highly favored it would be highly ungrateful in me were I to suffer this to dwell much on my mind.

But in the final letter, written December 5, 1812, one can hear the beginning of doubt, misgivings, anxiety, as if, too late, Maria Branwell is asking herself whether she is altogether wise in marrying a man she has known so short a time.

So you *thought* that *perhaps* I *might* expect to hear from you. As the case was so doubtful, and you were in such great haste, you might as well have deferred writing a few days longer, for you seem to suppose it is a matter of perfect indifference to me whether I hear from you or not. I believe I once requested you to judge of my feelings by your own—am I to think that *you* are thus indifferent? I feel very unwilling to entertain such an opinion, and am grieved that you should suspect me of such a cold, heartless attachment. But I am too serious on the subject; I only meant to rally you a little on the beginning of your last, and to tell you that I fancied there was a coolness in it which none of your former letters had contained."

Yes, she had truly fathomed the nature of the handsome, passionate, determined Irish lad who had spoken her so fair

27

at first, but was perhaps already disinterested. Was his love the love of a man who only woos to win, and having done so turns to pastures new or to his own affairs? If she was disturbed by such premonitions she was only too rightly disturbed. In her attempted gaiety of speech and manner there is deep pathos. She had been attracted by the flame as others had been before her, both men and women, and had flown headlong into it. A few short weeks of happiness, romance, dreams—that was all she had. Nine years later, having borne her husband six children in as many years, and as in duty bound, it was all over, for *her*. Yet the very fact of her motherhood has given her name meaning in its proudest sense. We all pray that we may be used to advance mankind through such creative potentialities as we may possess. Maria Brontë stands unique among those who created as it is ordained that women shall create.

*Chapter* v  ON THE WEST RIDING

THE WEST RIDING is the most famous part of England's largest county, Yorkshire County. Its moors rise a thousand feet above the valleys. They run forty miles east and west and a hundred and fifty north and south. In every direction they seem to roll off and over the edge of the world. A mood of desolation, like a waiting bird of prey, hovers above them, and never lifts even in bright sunlight. There are no woods patching its broad reaches; no blue lakes break the surface monotone of gray-green land. There are several rivers: the Aire, the Sheaf, and the Don. The big cities on the outskirts of the Riding are York, Leeds, and Sheffield. They are large industrial cities, using the rivers as their source of water power.

Looking across the moors on a clear day, one can see low mountains on the horizon's edge, but the moors themselves never lift above smoothly rolling hills. Here and there an outcrop of granite breaks at the crest of a hill; it was on such cragged promontories that the natives built their villages. These moorland towns are bare of orchards and gardens. Their stone cottages and church towers rise above lichened walls, gray and cold against the colder sky. So the total impression of the moors, spread out over Yorkshire's West Riding, is one of loneliness and indifference, of barren pride, of stubborn refusal to submit to fertility, in other words, of

29

nature gone underground. They only spring to life when the storms break, when rain or snow sweeps across them in blinding sheets, when the wind screams in the stone crevices and the twisted gullies of the sunken rivers. Then the dwellers on the moors, few and far between, are even more isolated from one another. The winter winds and rains hold them to their habitations, and nature takes over.

However, although the moors are regarded as an extensive wasteland, they are not without a muted life of their own. There are golden plover and red grouse in the brush; there are peewits crying low over the heather; and larks and linnets sing high above it all. The ground itself holds the moors' delicate outlines with carpets of green moss in the uneven stream beds, with heather clothing the roll of hills with a skintight dress of purple pink.

The seasons on the moors, except for winter, are no more than a promise of perfection. Spring is a "whisper down the field," summer is an Indian giver, and autumn has waved good-by from the road without coming in. Writing to Sydney Dobell, Charlotte Brontë said, "I know nothing of such an orchard country as you describe. I have never seen such a region. Our hills only confess the coming of summer by growing green with young fern and moss, and secret little hollows. Their bloom is reserved for autumn; then they burn with a kind of dark glow, differing, doubtless, from the blush of garden blossoms." And when she invited Mrs. Gaskell to visit the parsonage she also warned her, telling her she must only come "in the spirit which might sustain you in case you were setting out on a brief trip to the backwoods of America. Leaving civilization you must come out to barbarism, loneliness and liberty."

Yet by strange contrast the cities of this seemingly desolate

30

region, which Charlotte considered uncivilized, were among the first to give civilization the implements and goods necessary for our material progress. Perhaps such "progress" is not civilization! But be that as it may, long before the turn of the eighteenth century the West Riding had become a prosperous manufacturing center. Lancaster and Manchester on the western edge of the Riding produced enough cotton goods for the export trade. To the east, Sheffield and Leeds were making leather goods, glass, ironware, earthenware, woolens, and cottons. Around Bradford, in the heart of the moorland, lay the natural resources, coal, iron, stone, being quarried in sufficient amount for foreign trade. All this industrial ferment was well under way by the year 1820, the year Patrick Brontë moved his family into the parsonage in the village of Haworth.

Between York and Sheffield, in the northeast corner of the Riding, are clustered twelve or fifteen villages. Their names are poetry, and would be poetry whether Emily and Charlotte had rubbed them with Aladdin's lampdust or not. Keighley, Stanbury, Hatherage, Withens, Thornton, Birstall, Dewsbury, Cowan Bridge, Rawdon, Stonegappe—what names could come more quaintly to an English tongue? Haworth was one of them. And Haworth was to be the hearthstone where the wild hearts of three girls would make a light across the moors, across the world, as far as the written word has carried their names.

On coming down from Cambridge, Patrick Brontë became curate at Hartshead, in Yorkshire County, and remained there for four years after his marriage. During the following four years he was vicar at Thornton, moving to Haworth in 1820 where he was to remain until his death in 1861. The two elder children, Elizabeth and Maria, were born at Hartshead, the four younger, Charlotte, Branwell, Emily, and Anne, at Thornton.

The Brontë family already numbered eight when it moved from Thornton to Haworth in May or June of 1820. It was only a distance of six miles as the road winds, a distance they covered, even in the days of oxcarts, in a matter of a few hours. Yet somehow we have come to feel that those six miles represent far more than mere lineal distance, that they represent two worlds. Perhaps this is because, though the Brontës had been faced with the usual hardships of poverty and illness that were a part of the life of any poorly paid English vicar with a rapidly growing family, they had not met the acute sorrows that were to come to them at Haworth. For from the day they turned their six carts, filled with children and household goods, into the driveway of the Haworth parsonage, and entered the bleak, damp, stone house, darkness and death seemed to have entered with them. Yet it was out of that same pyre of grief and misfortune that the genius of the children was to rise like the phoenix flown, so that what was begun one day in Emdale Fort, when Patrick Brontë read *Paradise Lost* to the high heavens, came to its fruition in a little English village, a long way and a hard way from its Irish birthplace. Paradise had been lost and regained.

*Chapter* VI   THE WOODEN SOLDIERS

Much of the secret of the Brontë's genius lies in the writing they did as children, when they seriously played at being authors. These earliest stories and poems, letters and notes, have been so scattered, even lost, that students of the Brontës have been largely thwarted in their desire to get to the root of the creative forces at work in the Brontë home during the childhood of the three girls. Biographers who had the first access to the early manuscripts failed to make the use of them that their subsequent value would have inspired. Later the manuscripts were distributed among collectors and libraries. For instance, Mr. Clement Shorter, in behalf of Thomas J. Wise, an English bibliophile, purchased from Charlotte's widower, Mr. Arthur Bell Nichols, most of the Brontë papers and letters, including a package of stories written by the children. These stories and records were known to Mrs. Gaskell when she wrote her life of Charlotte. A considerable portion of this package of stories eventually fell into the hands of Mr. Henry H. Bonnell of Philadelphia, and came to this country. When Mr. Shorter disposed of his collection he gave a great deal of it to the British Museum, and smaller amounts to other collectors and to friends. In the same way, the collection bought by Mr. Bonnell, who recently died, was also scattered, the largest portion being presented to the Brontë Museum at Haworth, and certain manuscripts being sold.

Fannie E. Ratchford made the first thorough study of the youthful writing of the four Brontë children. Her book, *The Brontës' Web of Childhood,* is an illuminating piece of research among the manuscripts, which include a considerable number of tales, dramas, poems, and novelettes. For what was at one time being called "insignificant juvenilia" has since assumed the importance it deserves in an analysis of the nature and environment of the Brontë genius. On this very attitude of earlier biographers, Miss Ratchford charges: "It would seem that neither Mrs. Gaskell nor Mr. Shorter was equal to the forbidding and apparently interminable task of reading in chronological order the hundreds of pages of microscopic hand printing which guarded the secret of Charlotte's childhood and early womanhood. Thus they missed a record far more revealing of the mind and genius of their subject than the letters which they made the basis for their biographies, and a romance more interesting than the speculations that have gathered around the contradictory revelations of letters and manuscripts, and chose the more understandable one—the letters." *

Miss Ratchford's assertion that something was missed in the neglect of these youthful writings, which might throw light on the later work, is all too true. For during those formative years the Brontë children all seem to have given free rein to an imagination that escaped into a world of fancy. In spirit they moved away from the sadness and loneliness, the loss of a mother to the graveyard across the wall, of a father to a library behind closed doors and a closed heart,

* Reprinted from Fannie Elizabeth Ratchford, *The Brontës' Web of Childhood.* Copyright 1941 by Columbia University Press.

and went into a fairy realm where they played at storytelling as simply as other children play with dolls and kites. By this very token, that they entered into another world of illusion with so much naturalness and joy, with the excitement of secrecy and in the manner of playing a game with each other, it may be said that we are too prone to call their game an escape. Psychiatry may have put the word in our mouths, and psychiatry could be wrong.

Miss Ratchford, for one, discounts this accepted interpretation of the Brontës' childhood. "In contrast," she writes, "to the oft-repeated, tragic picture of the four little Brontës, frail, neglected, and prematurely old, crouching in terror before the ever-threatening monsters of disease and early death, the *juvenilia* show us singularly happy beings, possessed of an Aladdin's lamp through whose magic power they transcended time and distance, walked with kings, and swayed the destiny of mighty empires."

Yet "the tragic picture of the four little Brontës," so often told, is a story of fact and not of fancy. Life, *and* death, were too hard and too swift in their attack for children to take. A mother, the only individual who could hold the home to its spiritual shape, died when her eldest of six children was only eight; a father failed to be of solace in their time of need, much as he may have wanted to help. The house itself was a cheerless, poverty-stricken, unhealthy place, where sunlight and beauty never entered. It necessarily follows that these "singularly happy beings," as Miss Ratchford calls them, could not have been happy as children should be happy, running and playing and laughing in the love and security of parental care and encouragement. Any child of eager sensibilities, and these children were gifted with the greatest sensibility, could scarcely avoid an inward turning to the bright warmth of the imagination. Here they find a strength that keeps their minds and hearts from breaking. It is a talent in which children excel: a need for play finding a way to play. It is the parents that go into sanitariums.

The play within a play, into which the Brontë children "escaped," seems to have been begun on a June day in 1826. Mr. Brontë had been to Leeds on business, and when he returned he brought a present of wooden soldiers for little Branwell. Branwell shouted to his sisters to come and see the wonderful gift. Charlotte snatched a soldier from the box and said, "Oh, look, this is the Duke of Wellington. This shall be my Duke." So of course Emily chose a soldier for herself, and said it was to be called "Gravey." And Anne said hers would be "Waiting Boy." After that Branwell picked his favorite and named it "Buonaparte." From that day on the characters of the Duke, Gravey, Waiting Boy, and Buonaparte became the protagonists of an ever developing drama, filled with romantic enchantment and symbolic significance. "In these wooden soldiers," Miss Ratchford continues, "the children had at hand *dramatis personae* for an ever-lengthening series of games. And as the games progressed several conceptions tended to run together, and soldiers, literary men, artists, prophets, and rogues fused in a complex and representative society." A great deal of their game they secretly confided to little slips of paper. Writing the "inventions" down, and passing them from one to another when no one was observing them, seemed to add greatly to the creative excitement that had begun to take fire in the four children.

They culled many of their characters from their father's library. They invented towns and places. There was Dream Island, the Glass Town, and the Guinea Coast of Africa. They peopled the towns with heroes, famous names of the day.

The soldiers from which it all sprang took part in every episode, were present at every crisis, and were collectively called the "Young Men." Eventually the "Young Men" became the chroniclers, as well as the participants, of many a tale. As in *The Arabian Nights*, the authors became genii whose omnipotence gave them power over life and death.

The Brontë children, before and even during adolescence, made this writing into a game in which the materials were wholly of the mind and the emotions. The language in which they recorded and communicated the experiences of their "Young Men" is shot through with the same beauty and flame that ultimately was to crystallize into the superb romances of Charlotte's Angria and the Angrians, the epic naturalism of Emily's Gondal and the Gondalians. No better practice fields could be devised for the writing of such classics as *Jane Eyre* and *Wuthering Heights*.

*Chapter* VII   CHARLOTTE OF ANGRIA

AT TWENTY-THREE," Miss Ratchford says,
"Charlotte Brontë emerged from the strangest authorship
that ever an author served." That apprenticeship was in the
Angrian romances. Beginning with the *Young Men's Play*, inspired by the wooden soldiers, through countless ramifica-
tions of characters, scene, plot, and conflict, including the
Angrian period, Charlotte had spent thirteen years living
one life and writing another. Much of that time she had
written in collaboration with Branwell, but the Angrian stories are almost entirely of her own devising.

Although Branwell did not possess the genius his family
long believed him to have, he was a very important part of
the make-believe that inspired all four children. He had a
boy's technical and inventive sense, and "wars and rumors
of wars" were meat and drink to him. In all Branwell's contributions to the *Young Men's Play* there are battles and
campaigns, skillful maneuvers, plans of attack and retreat.
He also created the political issues, the motives and ambitions, that drive men to war. But his interest did not go
beyond military problems, action in the field, heroic deeds
with the sword, slaughter and blood, defeat and victory.
He was wholly absorbed in active combat. When he ran out
of nations to conquer, kingdoms to annex, he simply invented
new ones, farther and farther afield. He hadn't named his

38

wooden soldier "Buonaparte" for nothing. And it was Branwell, when the possibilities of any further development of the *Young Men's Play* seemed to be exhausted once and for all, who had Napoleon "invade the vast stretch of uncivilized jungleland lying to the east and southeast of Glass Town," the Young Men's capital. He arranged that an army under Arthur Wellesley, Marquis of Duoro, should meet and defeat the French Emperor. For this service to his country, Wellesley was to compel his father-in-law, the Earl of Northangerland, to request that the Parliament of Glass Town grant him the rich province of Angria, under the titles Duke of Zamora, King of Angria, and Emperor Adrian.

Angria, this new mythical empire, was located on the South Pacific coast of Africa. The idea for its location came from the Reverend J. Goldsmith's *A Grammar of General Geography,* a book the children used constantly in plotting their kingdoms. Branwell drew the specifications for the seven provinces of Angria, each with its own capital, lord lieutenant, and hierarchy of potentates. The Duke of Zamora and the Earl of Northangerland were to build Adrianapolis, the capital of the largest province and the seat of government for the kingdom. Branwell was the *deus ex machina.*

But, according to Miss Ratchford, "Charlotte shows little interest in the geography of the new country, its political organization and its financial resources, concerning herself solely with the spirit of the people." It might be said that she began to part company with Branwell when she wrote the "poem" she called "A National Ode for the Angrians." From that day she became increasingly more concerned with the spirit and destiny of a *people,* rather than with a nation's military prowess. The hero of her first Angrian stories was her soldier boy, the Duke of Wellington; but as the Angrian Empire grew and multiplied, she replaced Wellington with his son, Arthur Augustus Adrian Wellesley, Duke of Zamora and Marquis of Duora. To give Wellesley a background befitting his station in life she wrote a thirty-eight-thousand-word prologue, as it were, which bears the title "High Life in Verdopolis," dealing with its "lords and ladies and squires of high degree." Miss Ratchford calls this "a delightful orgy of Byronism."

It is obvious that Charlotte, as she approached young womanhood, was beginning to be more interested in the call of romance than in the call to arms. The Duke of Wellington, who won in battle, finally yielded to the Duke of Zamora, who won in love. Zamora is "irresistible to women." Mary Percy, the Queen, Maria Queachi, and Marian Hume, are all subject to his spell. And in Charlotte's portrayal of the "ladies" of Angria, the violence of their passions, the strength of their devotion and allegiance to lord and master, one can easily trace the descent of *Jane Eyre* and *Villette*. Here are the first intimations of a feminine psychology in which sacrifice and revolt are made the underlying principles of a woman's behavior when she loves all too well, if not always wisely.

Charlotte's Angrian "serial story" revolves entirely around the stormy emotional life of the Duke of Zamora. His adventures become so complicated, so intricate and entangled, that one doubts if there was any sequence intended. Charlotte was obviously not writing, or attempting, the novel form as yet. The events are episodic, the characters inconsistent. To add to the confusion, the Duke is given a dual personality. He is a Dr. Jekyll and Mr. Hyde. On one hand he slays the women, runs the gamut of the emotional scale from gaiety to melancholy, indulges in all the sensuous pleasures of court life, is involved in every amorous intrigue that Charlotte can imagine for him; on the other, he slays the enemy, is noble and patriotic, honored by his subjects for saving his country in its hour of need.

Even Charlotte would appear to have lost her way in the maze of incident and counterincident, character and lack of character, that takes her "down the labyrinthine ways" of her own mind. Now and then she pauses in the rush of anecdote to try to straighten her characters out, as well as herself. One such attempt, "Corner Dishes, Being a Small Collection of Mixed and Unsubstantial Trifles in Prose and Verse," is a hundred thousand words tossed off to explain by chapter and verse the true nature of Angria and its aristocracy. The "upper crust" society of Adrianapolis and the provincial capitals, the Duke and his friends, are sketched with the same strokes that an artist uses in working up to a masterpiece, the difference being that Charlotte never takes the entire responsibility for the sketches. There is always an alter ego. Every character, every incident, is described by still another character in the narrative itself. By such a method the author kills two birds with one stone, giving us a picture of the narrator as well as his subject. She brings her early heroes and heroines to Angria, but often in name only. Once they have become Angrians their personalities may suffer a sea change. As, for instance, the Rogue, who was a villain in the Glass Town cycle, cruel and treacherous, turns up in Angria as Alexander Percy, Earl of Northangerland, father-in-law of the Duke of Zamora, and a man of integrity and honor as well as substance.

In the meantime, Charlotte's devotion to Branwell, her love and admiration for him, was undergoing a severe strain. Branwell was going astray. He was not only becoming a familiar of Haworth's Black Bull Tavern, and drinking to excess, but in other ways he was indulging in habits that were to pave the way to his downfall. Charlotte was distressed and worried. No amount of expostulation or threatening seemed to move Branwell. In fact he became the more perverse as his sisters remonstrated with him. And it may easily have been a desire to influence him indirectly that gave Charlotte the idea of caricaturing him in her stories. For Patrick Benjamin Wiggins, met one day by Lord Charles Wellesley (Charlotte's favorite raconteur) as he makes his call on the Queen, is quite obviously Branwell. " 'My readers,' declares Lord Charles, 'will have recognized Patrick Benjamin Wiggins, that quizzical little personage whose outré manners, and almost insane devotion to all the celebrated characters in Verdopolis, have of late absorbed so much of public attention. His form is that of a lad of sixteen, his face that of a man of twenty-five, his hair is red, his features not bad, for he has a Roman nose, small mouth, and well-turned chin; his figure too, though diminutive, is perfectly symmetrical, and of this he seems not unconscious. A pair of spectacles garnishes his nose, and through these he is constantly gazing at Flanagan (Zamora's boxing master), whose breadth of shoulder appears to attract his sincere admiration, as every now and then he touched his own with the tip of his forefinger, and pushed · out his small contracted chest to make it appear broader.' " Miss Ratchford rather doubts that Charlotte is as yet fully aware of the "ruinous tendencies of her brother's village associations," since the portrait of him as Patrick Wiggins is done "without condemnations, in good-natured, teasing satire."

However, the following passage, taken from Lord Charles's narration, would indicate that Charlotte was truly concerned over her brother's wayward attitude.

"I'm rather thirsty," Branwell remarks to Lord Charles, "and I think I'll call for a pot of porter or a tumbler of brandy and water at the public yonder." What he has there is tea and bread and butter, but he returns lying and boasting: "I feel like a lion now, at any rate. Two bottles of Sneachi's Glass Town ale, and a double quart of porter, with cheese, bread and cold beef, have I devoured since I left you, Lord Charles, and I am not a bit touched, only light and smart and active. I'd defy all the danders in Christendom now—that I would! and a hundred goslings to boot. What were you asking me, sir?"

"I have asked you where you were born, sir, and now I ask what relations you have?"

"Why, in a way I may be said to have no relations. I can't tell you who my father and mother were, no more than that stone. I've some people who call themselves akin to me in the shape of three girls. They are honored by possessing me as a brother, but I deny that they are my sisters."

"What are your sisters' names?"

"Charlotte Wiggins, Emily Jane Wiggins, and Anne Wiggins."

"Are they as queer as you?"

"Oh, they are miserable, silly creatures, not worth talking about. Charlotte's eighteen years old, a broad, dumpy thing, whose head does not come higher than my elbow. Emily's sixteen, lean and scant, with a face the size of a penny; and Anne's nothing, absolutely nothing."

"What! Is she an idiot?"

"Next door to it."

"Humph! You're a pretty set."

This dialogue is extremely revealing in many ways. It makes it clear that Branwell's lack of physical stature may

43

have had a great deal to do with his becoming a wastrel, and particularly with his fondness for drink. For the latter made him feel aggressive, bold and pugnacious. It drowned out the inferiority complex, the feeling that they were "nobody" as a family, and he was "nobody" as a man. The conversation discloses, on the other hand, an opposite trait in Charlotte: the saving grace that allows her to poke fun at herself. That nice balance of nature which makes it possible for us to laugh at ourselves, and see ourselves as others see us, is particularly necessary in a writer. Charlotte, Emily, and Anne all had it to a degree that saved them. Branwell was without it, and he paid the price.

The Angrian cycle draws to a close in 1839. The Duke of Zamora is overthrown in the course of a revolution, and, suspecting the queen of playing a part in the conspiracy that led to the rebellion, he murders her. He is promptly exiled. But the Angrians rally under Warner Howard Warner, scion of an ancient Angrian clan, and defeat the usurpers, restoring Zamora to the throne. Whereupon Charlotte introduces a new narrator, Charles Townshend, a younger son of the Duke of Wellington, and the Angrian cycle ends triumphantly with two outstanding narratives, one entitled "Passing Events," and the other bearing no name. The last is a long poem written in the stanza form of Byron's *Don Juan*. It is a glowing account of the restoration of the kingdom and Zamora's return to the throne, with the late-murdered Queen Mary at his side. Mary, Duchess of Zamora, Queen of Angria, has been Charlotte's favorite heroine, and she could not leave her in the grave! She restores her to life, to the throne, and to her husband's love and protection.

"With the end of the Angrian War," as Miss Ratchford says, "Charlotte's awakening was complete, and conditions set for the maturing of her genius; fancy had given way to an intensity of imagination that carried with it a suggestion of the supernatural; suffering had changed adolescent romanticism to passion so strong as to give the stamp of conviction to the most impossible situations; and mere fluency of expression had developed into a characteristic style."

## *Chapter* VIII   EMILY OF GONDAL

THE enigma of Emily Brontë's genius lies in the Gondal writings, which in turn grew out of the same play instinct that she shared in common with her brother and sisters. The actual writing is as enigmatic as the spirit that produced it. In comparison, Charlotte's progress can be followed quite easily as she steadily improved in craftsmanship, as she grew in literary stature, from childhood through adolescence into young womanhood. The *Young Men's Play*, the "Glass Town" adventures, and the Angrian romances spell out her steps. But with Emily we are continually baffled by evasions and reservations until we are rewarded with the perfected accomplishments of her poetry and the novel.

Most of what we know about Emily as a person, during the early years, has had to be gathered at second hand from Charlotte, Anne, and Branwell. And *all* that we know about her writing during the same period must be discovered from a few slight compositions that were overlooked in the wholesale destruction of her manuscripts. Whether Emily herself destroyed them, or Charlotte, as has been claimed, the result is devastatingly the same. Nothing is left for us to study but a letter, a birthday note, a scrap of diary, and five papers in French which she wrote as a class assignment at the Heger Pensionnat in Brussels.

Yet it stands to reason that the novel, *Wuthering Heights,* and the volume of poems, did not spring full-fledged from her brain as Minerva from the forehead of Jupiter. Emily in all probability wrote as extensively as the other three children. She must have contributed her share to the *Young Men's Play* and "Glass Town." And it is perhaps doubly unfortunate that Emily's early contributions to the imaginative structure they built should have been lost. The very purpose of its destruction could have been the very reason we would find it most valuable: that it revealed more truth than make-believe, that it explained the Brontë family as Charlotte and Branwell were either unable, or unwilling, to unveil it. An analysis of Emily's character, as we get glimpses of it in her finished work, would indicate that she must have understood the psychological implications in human relationships far better than the others. Although younger than Charlotte and Branwell, she may have been more touched in spirit by the misunderstandings of her parents, her mother's unspoken loneliness and untimely death, the loss of the two older sisters, her father's retirement into "a shell of silence," and she may have been more aware than Charlotte of Branwell's disintegration and defection. She may even have given Charlotte away, as well as herself, in the matter of their attachment to M. Heger, "the Professor" of the school in Brussels. So that if it was Charlotte who destroyed the evidence, one can see how she might have been tempted. But the loss of what Emily trusted to paper is a cruel one in terms of literary history.

There are many indications that Emily did not see eye to eye with the other three in the treatment of character and plot in the *Young Men's Play* and "Glass Town." The puppets with which Branwell and Charlotte stuffed their kingdoms

47

to overflowing were victims of circumstances in a prescribed world, a world of circumstances prescribed by Branwell and Charlotte. Through it all Emily appears to have been more inclined to ideas, and to the development of ideas into a formalized, definite philosophy. While Branwell built cities, she charted human values. Emily's nature would seem to be rooted in the primal myth of creation, in its divine mystery. She was already something of a mystic.

Emily and Charlotte began to go separate ways, in the spiritual sense, once they were launched on their Angrian and Gondal "epics." As Charlotte and Branwell discovered Angria, Emily and Anne immediately set up a kingdom of their own, possibly in a spirit of rivalry. Gondal, an island continent in the North Pacific (Angria was in the South Pacific), was very similar in many of its physical characteristics, its wars and conquests, to Angria—as was quite natural in view of the friendly competition between the Emily-Anne Charlotte-Branwell romances at that time. And there were only minor differences in the geographic and economic patterns of the two empires. Angria, as we have said, was established as an independent state by a Glass Town act of Parliament, under the Duke of Zamora, and was made up of seven provinces ruled by lord lieutenants of the realm. Gondal, on the other hand, had nine kingdoms and provinces, the provinces being ruled by viceroys. There are revolutions, counter-revolutions; thrones fall and are restored; men rise to power only to die the death. But beyond this the similarity ends. For, although the Queen, Augusta Geraldine Almeda, is a female counterpart of the Duke of Zamora, she possesses the strange and divine mystery of the earth. The goddess motif enters the picture. One has a feeling that Greek mythology must have had a strong influence on Emily.

48

Anne had very little part in the construction of Gondal, and still less in its destiny. Beyond place names, geographic locations, and setting up the machinery of government (more or less copying Branwell in the process), Anne left the shaping of incident and character to Emily. As Emily reached down into the subconscious, plumbing the dark mysteries and bright enchantments that were beginning to seethe in her, Anne was left far behind. As Emily's spirit soared above mere plot and adventure into the creative imagination that shapes life into art, Anne hung more and more on Emily's words and wrote less and less herself. Anne remained Emily's devoted and admiring apostle, urging Emily not to forget her Gondal people, anxiously awaiting the next installment.

Meanwhile, in the summer of 1836, Emily's writing took still another turn. She began to write the Gondal story in verse, in a series of poems filled with intense passion, in which love and liberty are the burning symbols. There are two strands of creative force woven into the action of the Gondal poetry. One deals primarily with the life revolving in and about the Palace of Instruction, an institution embodying the social and civic virtues, the social ideals, of Gondalian society; the other dealing with the stormy joys and sorrows of the royal lovers, Julius Benzaida and Queen Augusta Geraldine Almeda, and their enemies Lady Angelica and Douglas. Bitter civil strife between two political factions, the Royalists and the Republicans, keeps the country in constant turmoil. And against a brilliant tapestry of love and war the character of Queen Almeda, Emily's chief protagonist, changes, declares Miss Ratchford, from that of a "beautiful and richly endowed queen, a generous, happy girl, hardening through indulgence of an ardent nature, into a

49

selfish, cruel woman ruthlessly feeding her vanity on the souls of men."

The Gondal tale, unfolding as it does by lyric and ballad, instead of by narrative verse, has no clear sequence of time or event. It is therefore extremely difficult to follow. But actually it has ceased to be important, except to the research worker who desires to trace the fountain sources of Emily's inspiration, whether or not we can read the Gondal poetry as a history of Gondal. Because many of the individual poems are immortal, they are enough to make the name of Emily Brontë immortal. "Remembrance," a dirge for a love long dead; "The Wanderer from the Fold," a lament for a moral derelict, probably written with Branwell in mind; "No Coward Soul Is Mine," an expression of her own indomitable courage; "The Visionary" and "The Prisoner," in which the mystic speaks from the soul; and many others proving Emily's oneness with nature have a permanent place in our literature. It is unnecessary for the reader to attempt to comprehend the entire Gondal manuscript, which is wholly unintelligible in the mass, filled as it is with murder and suicide, captivity and betrayal, war and pestilence. Much of it is the dross remaining as childhood and adolescence burn away, leaving the bright prophetic sparks of pure art.

*Chapter* IX   THE SMOLDERING INTERVAL

THE last of Charlotte's Angrian stories, written in the year 1839, were "Henry Hastings" and "Caroline Hernon." Anne, in a letter dated 1841, says that she is at work on "Solala Vernon's Life," while all we know of Emily at this time, without the evidence of a single extant manuscript, is that she had ceased to write the Gondal epic in prose and was secretly writing it in verse. Branwell, in the meantime, had quite definitely turned from literature to the art that was to prove a dismal failure.

The three sisters had come through an apprenticeship in writing that cannot be matched in literary annals, and with no self-consciousness of what it could and would mean for their future. Professional authorship as a career was scarcely to be hoped for by women, least of all women of their status in the English society of that day. However, it seems to have crossed Charlotte's mind as early as 1836, as is witnessed by her letter to Robert Southey in December of that year. And in January, 1837, Branwell wrote to Wordsworth, sending him excerpts from a story he expected to develop into a long narrative. These letters were a pitiful reaching out for attention and encouragement from the contemporary authors whom they read and admired from a distance, men already appreciated by a large public. But, whatever the Brontës hoped, the seven years from 1839 to 1846, when the *Poems* were published, were a smoldering interval during which the fire of their genius was banked down, though it never ceased to burn. May Sinclair says that it was the impressions they took in during those years that assured their immortality.

They left Haworth several times during this period, going as students to Brussels or as governesses to the manor houses of Yorkshire. They were separated from each other, something that must have been acutely difficult to bear after the close, even mystical, bonds forged between them during the years of association in their childhood literary partnership. Already they were individuals, uncommonly perceptive, uncommonly sensitive, and it is not so strange that the experiences of the outside world were to be screened, through what one might call a kind of clairvoyance, into an essence of creative insight. And it is in her voluminous letters to Ellen Nussey, and her briefer correspondence with Mary Taylor, that Charlotte Brontë has left us an extensive record of the impressions made on her by the places and persons of another world than Haworth.

Emily and Anne were seeing the world, too, through other eyes than Charlotte's. Their impressions were colored and tempered by the deep imprint the moods and mystery of the moors had long since made on their hearts. For the two younger sisters felt a stronger kinship to the wild beauty of Yorkshire's West Riding than Charlotte had ever felt. Even when Charlotte wrote her "prose hymn" to the earth, in *Shirley*, it was Emily speaking through her. It was Emily who understood that only freedom of communion with nature can establish a bond between the temporal and the eternal. During her brief and infrequent absences from Haworth, Emily became the more convinced that mankind is what fails man; that man must turn inward to his own soul to be sustained; that only nature can give him the faith to live; that men cannot rely on each other to achieve a common goal of happiness.

During the years 1839 to 1846, as we have said, the yeast of experience was beginning to have its effect on the Brontë genius, causing it to turn, as it were. There is a distinct change in the tone of Charlotte's letters to Ellen Nussey. Something creeps into them that is almost fey, a spirit of wildness that might burst from its crysalis at any moment. One such letter bears quoting in full for its charming play with words:

"The wind bloweth where it listeth. Thou hearest the sound thereof, but cannot tell whence it cometh, nor whither it goeth." That I believe, is Scripture, though in what chapter or book, or whether it be correctly quoted, I can't possibly say. However, it behooves me to write a letter to a young woman of the name of E., with whom I was once acquainted, "in life's morning march, when my spirit was young." This young woman wished me to write her some time since, though I have nothing to say—I e'en put it off, day by day, till at last, fearing that she will "curse me by her gods," I feel constrained to sit down and tack a few lines together, which she may call a letter or not as she pleases. Now if the young woman expects sense in this production, she will find herself miserably disappointed. I shall dress her a dish of salmagundi—I shall cook a hash—compound a stew—toss up an *omelette soufflée à la Française,* and send it to her with my respects. The wind, which is very high up in our hills of Judea, though I suppose, down in the Philistine flats of B. parish it is nothing to speak of, has produced the same effects on the contents of my knowledge-box that a quaigh

53

of usequebaugh does upon those of most other bipeds.
I see everything *couleur de rose,* and am strongly inclined
to dance a jig, if I knew how. I think I must partake of a
pig or an ass—both animals are strongly affected by a high
wind. From what quarter the wind blows I cannot tell,
for I never could in my life; but I should very much like
to know how the great brewing-tub of Bridlington Bay
works, and what sort of yeastly froth rises just now on the
waves.

Of the three sisters, Charlotte had the most worldly experience in "the years between." In 1839 she had two proposals of marriage. She passed through the crucial and critical interlude at the Heger Pensionnat in Brussels. She tasted
humiliation as a governess in the home of the Sidgwicks at
Stonegappe, and later with Mrs. White at Rawdon. All this,
coming so closely after the imaginative saturation in the
Angrian romances, which were still echoing in her spirit,
must have affected her powerfully, though perhaps less
severely than similar experiences were to affect Emily and
Anne. At least Charlotte (hear Charlotte tell it in her letters!)
was never as homesick, as overcome with nostalgia for Haworth, as were the two younger girls. Ellen Nussey, and
even Mr. Williams, heard a great deal from Charlotte about
the unhappiness of Emily and Anne when away from home.
Their acute misery when cut off from the moors and the
winds of Yorkshire was as much a subject for Charlotte's
voluminous letter writing as were her own aches and pains,
though there is a surplus of the latter, also. Charlotte might
well be called a hypochondriac, and yet her obsession with
matters of health is most natural when one considers the
family's propensity to serious illness.

Emily was only away from Yorkshire during the eight

months' stay in Brussels, in 1842. Her school days at Cowan Bridge and Roe Head were behind her then, as were the six months she spent as a teacher in Halifax. In her preface to the posthumous edition of Emily's works, Charlotte describes the Brussels experience in its effect on Emily:

> After the age of twenty, having meantime studied alone with diligence and perseverance, she went with me to an establishment on the continent. The same suffering and conflict ensued, heightened by the strong recoil of her upright heretic and English spirit from the gentle Jesuitry of the foreign and Romish system. Once more she seemed sinking, but this time she rallied through the mere force of resolution: with inward remorse and shame she looked back on her former failure, and resolved to conquer, but victory cost her dear. She was never happy till she carried her hard-won knowledge back to the remote English village, the old parsonage-house, and desolate Yorkshire hills.

I have referred elsewhere to the five essays that Emily wrote in French as a class assignment at the Pensionnat. These have been lately translated for the first time, and published by the University of Texas. They are, as Miss Ratchford says in her foreword to the collection, "in a very real sense autobiographical, sketching the fullest and clearest self-portrait we have of Emily." In one of them, "A Letter from One Brother to Another," Emily reveals the agony of her exile even more poignantly than Charlotte had done it for her:

> I have crossed the ocean; I have traveled in several countries; I have been the poorest of the poor, ill among strangers without being able to offer the works of my hands in exchange for the bread that I was eating. Some-

time I have enjoyed luxuries and all the pleasures that they can afford their possessor, but always alone, always friendless, with no one to love me. I never thought of being reconciled with you, however. I did not want to enjoy again that concord of soul, that sweet and calm happiness of our childhood. Or if that thought came to me sometimes, I drove it out of my mind as unworthy and degrading weakness.

At last my soul and body being worn out with wandering, my bark shaken with so many tempests, I longed to gain a harbor. I resolved to end my days where they had begun, and I longed to see again the native heath and the home so long abandoned.*

I should like to repeat, and italicize, a sentence from this letter which seems to me to express the deepest core of what it was that made Emily so miserably unhappy away from Haworth: *"I have been . . . ill among strangers without being able to offer the works of my hands in exchange for the bread that I was eating."* It was the household duties she missed most urgently, the work that gave her a sense of usefulness and fulfillment in the community, and in the parsonage itself. Helping Tabby in the kitchen, kneading bread and peeling potatoes, washing and ironing, sweeping and dusting the beloved rooms, these were the acts that focused the hands and the heart into an excuse for being. It is not strange then that in faraway Brussels, as she dreamed of the "remote English village" and the "desolate Yorkshire hills," all the impressions that swept upon her in the midst of a busy school life in a foreign land should have distilled into the cry, "I long to gain a harbor!" She had already mapped and charted a

* "A Letter from One Brother to Another" by Emily Brontë is reprinted from *Five Essays by Emily Brontë* with the permission of the Walter Marion Manly III Publication Fund.

harbor on the coast of Eternity, and the craft that was to carry her there was built, hull, sails, and compass, out of the native heath and home without which she would have been lost in the sea of life.

As for Anne, she was in some ways more responsive to the faintest currents of emotion than her sisters. During her impressionable years, she was for a long time governess at the Robinson home in Thorp Green, where Branwell joined her as tutor of the Robinson boys. It was here she felt the barbs of cruel condescension and callous indifference that were to be the motif of her first novel. "She waited in silence and resignation," May Sinclair wrote, "and then told her own story in *Agnes Grey*." She was also more hurt, more deeply wounded, by Branwell's failure to live up to all his sisters had trusted him to be. It was Anne who took it upon her conscience to blame herself, more perhaps than Branwell, for his maladjustment and breakdown. Hence we have *The Tenant of Wildfell Hall;* as if she owed the world an example in order that others might steer a better course. Anne had schooled herself to a fortitude only matched by Emily's. But she had done it in travail, in the secret regions of her soul, where she battled with, even against, her destiny. Anne had fallen in love with the sea at first sight. It answered something fundamental in her character. It was therefore only fitting that she should die within the sound of its breakers.

*Chapter* x   CHARLOTTE

CHARLOTTE BRONTË was born at Thornton, in the Yorkshire West Riding, on April 21, 1816. When she was four years old, Patrick Brontë became curate of Haworth; and Haworth parsonage was to be Charlotte's home for the rest of her life, until her death at thirty-nine. Maria Brontë died very shortly after the family moved to Haworth, and the six children were, to all intents and purposes, left orphans. Mr. Brontë was not a natural father, any more than he had been a natural husband. Disappointed in his dreams of one day being a name in scholastic and literary pursuits, or in the church itself, bound down by the burdens and responsibilities of multiple parenthood, while seeming to experience none of its joys, Patrick Brontë had become a dour, God-fearing man who retired into his lonely study and his own thoughts for what cold comfort life still afforded him. His motherless children were shut out, silenced, and left to grow up as best they could. The eldest, Maria, became the "little mother" of the parsonage. She was sweet and good by nature, and accepted the overwhelming responsibility of caring for the five younger children in a way that would have done credit to someone much older. She even taught the little ones to read and write. Though Mr. Brontë made some attempt to hear the children's lessons, the teaching and preparation fell to Maria. It is reasonable to believe that the work and anxiety, the strain and undernourishment, of the years following their mother's death paved the way for the tuberculosis that took the two oldest, Maria and Elizabeth, at the ages of twelve and eleven, and Emily and Anne at thirty-one and thirty.

Shortly after Mrs. Brontë's death, Tabitha Ackroyd, a middle-aged woman from Haworth village, came into the household to help with the menial tasks. This was the famous Tabby, the Tabby who appears under various guises—Nelly Dean, Rachel, Mrs. Pryor—in the novels of Emily, Charlotte, and Anne. Charlotte and her sisters truly loved Tabby. They had a great respect for Aunt Elizabeth, Maria's sister, who came eventually to live with them, but they did not love her as they loved Tabby. Aunt Elizabeth was not their kind. She could never understand how her nieces could prefer books to pretty clothes, running on the moors to the society of other children. She was painstaking in her attempts to teach them sewing and embroidery and knitting. And in these homely arts Charlotte was her most apt pupil, acquiring a skill that stood her in great stead in later years when she went out in service, as governess or companion.

Charlotte's childhood, until she went to school at Cowan Bridge in 1824, in no way differed outwardly from that of her sisters and brother. She listened, as they did, to Maria's reading aloud of the Leeds *Intelligencer,* and discussed public affairs, and the important names of the day, with a gravity beyond her years. Though there were books in their father's study which the children were allowed to read, and the Leeds newspaper and *Blackwood's Magazine* came to the parsonage regularly, there were no toys, no dolls or art materials—until the advent of the wooden soldiers—to waken childish fancies or stir creative activities. Beauty, of color or shape, was lacking in the dark house. What the children found of these was on the moors. The wild countryside was their true nursery. Their father completely discouraged association with the village children, for what reason it is difficult to say. Was it because, remembering his own peasant childhood, he wanted to avoid contact with it? Did he feel he had so risen above his class that he preferred his children never to know its vulgarity, its ignorant prejudice and superstition?

In 1824, Charlotte and Emily followed Maria and Elizabeth in attendance at the Reverend Carus Wilson's School at Cowan Bridge, founded for the daughters of poor clergymen. The bad conditions of the school, sanitary and dietary, brought the older girls down with fevers, which their frail constitutions could not overcome, and soon after their withdrawal in the spring of 1825, both Maria and Elizabeth died. Charlotte remained at the school for less than a year, but it left an indelible impression on the child of eight, as we know from her description of Lowood School in *Jane Eyre*. It is interesting that her school report is still extant: "She writes indifferently. Ciphers a little and works neatly. Knows nothing of grammar, geography, history, or accomplishments. Altogether clever for her age, but knows nothing systematically."

After the tragic illness and death of Maria and Elizabeth, which were largely due, as noted above, to the desperately unhealthy and miserable conditions at Cowan Bridge, Mr. Brontë withdrew Charlotte and Emily in June of 1825, and for the next six years Charlotte studied at home under her father and Aunt Elizabeth. At fifteen she again went away to school, this time to Miss Wooler's School at Roe Head, which lies between Leeds and Huddersfield, less than twenty miles from Haworth. Mrs. Gaskell describes Charlotte at that time as "a quiet, thoughtful girl, very small in figure ('stunted' was the word she applied to herself), but her limbs and head were in just proportion to her slight, fragile body." She had "soft, thick brown hair, and peculiar eyes," Mrs. Gaskell goes on to say, "which I find it difficult to describe. They were large and well-shaped, their color a reddish brown, but if the iris was closely examined it appeared to be composed of a variety of tints. The usual expression was one of quiet, listening intelligence, but now and then, on some just occasion for vivid interest or wholesome indignation, a light would shine out, as if some spiritual lamp had been kindled, which glowed behind those expressive orbs. I never saw the like in any human creature. As for the rest of her features, they were plain, large and ill-set, but unless you began to catalogue them you were hardly aware of the fact, for the eyes and power of the countenance over-balanced every physical defect; the crooked mouth and the large nose were forgotten, and the whole face arrested the attention. . . . Her hands and feet were the smallest I ever saw. When one of the former was placed in mine it was like the soft touch of a bird in the middle of my palm. The delicate long fingers had a peculiar fineness of sensation, which was one reason why all her handiwork, of whatever kind—writing, sewing, knitting—was so clear and minute. She was remarkably neat in her whole personal attire, dainty as to the fit of her shoes and gloves."

At Miss Wooler's School, Charlotte made her first friends outside the family circle, two of them, Ellen Nussey and Mary Taylor, becoming lifelong friends. The voluminous correspondence resulting from these friendships, particularly with Ellen Nussey, has been the one most important means whereby we discover Charlotte as she thought and felt in the obscure years of her childhood and adolescence. Miss Wooler herself, though beginning as Charlotte's teacher, was to prove, in affection and devotion, more a mother than anyone Charlotte had known since the loss of her own.

Charlotte spent the better part of a year and a half at Miss Wooler's School, and her shortcomings, as recorded on the Cowan Bridge report card, were quickly observed at Roe Head. Both Ellen Nussey and Mary Taylor, in after years, were to comment on her lack of rudimentary and systematic knowledge, but they said she had a fund of general information, a wide reading in literature, a familiarity with public affairs, that were the envy of her fellow students. She also won a reputation as a storyteller, revealing her Irish heritage in a slight brogue remarked by Mary Taylor. As Mary wrote Mrs. Gaskell:

> We thought her very ignorant, for she had never learnt grammar at all, and very little geography.... But she would confound us by knowing things that were out of our range altogether. She was acquainted with most of the short pieces of poetry that we had to learn by heart; would tell us the authors, the poems they were taken from, and sometimes repeat a page or two. She had a habit of writing in italics (printing characters), and said she had learnt it by writing in their magazine. They brought out a "magazine" once a month, and wished it to look as like print as possible. She told us a tale out of it. No one wrote in it, and no one read it, but herself, her brother, and two sisters. She promised to show me some of these magazines, but retracted afterwards, and would never be persuaded to do so. In our play hours she sate, or stood still, with a book if possible. Some of us once urged her to be on our side in a game at ball. She said she had never played, and could not play. We made her try,

but soon found that she could not see the ball, so we put her out. She took all our proceedings with pliable indifference, and always seemed to need a previous resolution to say "no" to anything. She used to go and stand under the trees in the playground, and say it was pleasanter. She endeavoured to explain this, pointing out the shadows, the peeps of sky, etc. We understood but little of it. She said that at Cowan Bridge she used to stand in the burn, on a stone, to watch the water flow by. I told her she should have gone fishing; she said she never wanted to. She always showed physical feebleness in everything. She ate no animal food at school. It was about this time I told her she was very ugly. Some years afterwards, I told her I thought I had been very impertinent. She replied, "You did me a great deal of good, Polly, so don't repent of it!"

Charlotte left Roe Head in June of 1832, and her correspondence with Ellen Nussey began as soon as she had returned to Haworth parsonage. Mrs. Gaskell remarks on the absence of hope which, she says, forms "such a strong characteristic in Charlotte." In a letter dated July 21, 1832, Charlotte describes her daily life: "An account of one day is an account of all. In the morning, from nine o'clock till half past twelve, I instruct my sisters, and draw; then we walk till dinner-time. After dinner I sew till tea-time, and after tea I either write, read, or do a little fancy work, or draw, as I please. Thus, in one delightful, though somewhat monotonous course, my life is passed. I have been only out twice to tea since I came home. We are expecting company this afternoon, and on Tuesday next we shall have all the female teachers of the Sunday School to tea." One cannot but be struck by the omission of any reference to *what* she was writing, for we do know that the *Young Men's Play* and the Angrian romances, in which she had been engaged before going to Roe Head, had been resumed as soon as she returned, and were to be continued during the next three years until her return to Miss Wooler's School as a teacher.

When Charlotte did return to Miss Wooler's School, this time to teach, Emily accompanied her as a pupil. But Emily only remained three months. She was desperately unhappy and homesick during this brief interlude away from the parsonage, and was rapidly failing in health and spirit when Charlotte fortunately intervened to have her called home. Writing of the episode, though in retrospect, Charlotte showed a concern and affection for her younger sister that is most admirable and most touching. It does, in fact, reveal a quality of Charlotte's character that is essential in an understanding of her whole nature, and therefore bears quoting:

My sister Emily loved the moors. Flowers brighter than the rose bloomed in the blackest of the heath for her; —out of a sullen hollow in a livid hill-side, her mind could make an Eden. She found in the bleak solitude many and dear delights; and not the least and best-loved was—liberty. Liberty was the breath of Emily's nostrils; without it she perished. The change from her home to a school, and from her own very noiseless, very secluded, but unrestricted and unartificial mode of life, to one of disciplinary routine (though under the kindest auspices), was what she failed in enduring. Her nature proved here too strong for her fortitude. Every morning, when she woke, the vision of home and the moors rushed on her, and darkened and saddened the day that lay before her. Nobody knew what ailed her but me. I knew only too well. In this struggle her health was quickly broken: her white face, attenuated form, and failing strength, threatened rapid decline. I felt in my heart she would die, if she did not go home, and with this conviction obtained her recall.

It is clear that at nineteen Charlotte was already assuming the family leadership. Someone certainly needed to step into a breach that had never been satisfactorily filled since the death of Mrs. Brontë. Charlotte felt that the need was there, and tried her best to remedy the situation. It made her overly anxious, and overly aggressive, for her age. For instance, this first important step into taking family affairs into her own hands produced a crisis that almost ended her great friendship with Miss Wooler. After seeing that Emily was taken home, she brought Anne to the school instead. But Anne also became very ill there, and Charlotte thought Miss Wooler took her illness far too lightly. If it had not been for Miss Wooler's good sense, and mature emotional under-standing of Charlotte's attitude, there would undoubtedly have been an end of a fine relationship, the sort of rela-tionship Charlotte herself needed in all its aspects. But even though there was a reconciliation of sorts, there was never again the same warmth of trust that had previously existed. Charlotte's championship of Anne, her anger over Miss Wooler's apparent neglect of a serious matter, burned so deeply that it was to be the cause, much later, of Charlotte's refusal to take the school when Miss Wooler wished to retire. Her letter to Ellen Nussey at the time of the misunderstand-ing indicates how deeply she was affected:

> You were right in your conjectures respecting the cause of my sudden departure. Anne continued wretchedly ill, neither the pain nor the difficulty of breathing left her, and how could I feel otherwise than very miserable. I looked on her case in a different light to what I could

wish or expect any uninterested person to view it in. Miss Wooler thought me a fool, and by way of proving her opinion treated me with marked coolness. We came to a little éclaircissement one evening. I told her one or two rather plain truths, which set her a-crying; and the next day, unknown to me, she wrote papa, telling him that I had reproached her bitterly, taken her severely to task, etc. Papa sent for us the day after he had received her letter. Meantime I had formed a firm resolution to quit Miss Wooler and her concerns for ever; but just before I went away, she took me to her room, and giving way to her feelings, which in general she restrains far too rigidly, gave me to understand that in spite of her cold, repulsive manners, she had a considerable regard for me, and would be very sorry to part with me. If any body likes me, I cannot help liking them; and remembering that she had in general been very kind to me, I gave in and said I would come back if she wished me. So we are settled again for the present, but I am not satisfied. I should have respected her far more if she had turned me out of doors, instead of crying for two days and two nights together. I was in a regular passion; my "*warm* temper" quite got the better of me, of which I don't boast, for it is a weakness; nor am I ashamed of it, for I had reason to be angry.

Anne is now much better, though she still requires a great deal of care. However, I am relieved from my worst fears respecting her. I approve highly of the plan you mention, except as it regards committing a verse of the Psalms to memory. I do not see the direct advantage to be derived from that. We have entered on a new year. Will it be stained as darkly as the last with all our sins, follies, secret vanities, and uncontrolled passions and propensities? I trust not; but I feel in nothing better, neither humbler nor purer. It will be three weeks next

Monday to the termination of the holidays. Come to see me, dear Ellen, as soon as you can; however bitterly I sometimes feel towards other people, the recollection of your mild, steady friendship consoles and softens me. I am glad you are not such a passionate fool as myself.

Meanwhile, Emily had taken a teaching position at Law Hill, near Halifax, where her general duties were so difficult as to make her, in Charlotte's opinion, "a slave." Also the anxiety over Branwell's future was becoming critical, so that when Charlotte left Miss Wooler's she made up her mind to put the family exchequer on a substantial footing. How else, except by what they earned, could Branwell achieve his destiny? Charlotte's faith in Branwell's genius was as yet unimpaired. But for the daughters of a poor clergyman in the early Victorian era the field of employment was definitely limited. One could be a teacher or a governess, a governess or a teacher. A governess was a combination of nursemaid, seamstress, and teacher. But she had tried teaching, and though many of the associations at Miss Wooler's had been pleasant and beneficial, yet she was wearied in spirit by the attempt to inculcate the young with knowledge, infuse them with ambition. So she now decided to try the only other alternative, that of being a governess in a family, although she had an intense dislike for very young children where discipline was a necessary part of the routine.

In April, 1839, she sent Anne off to Mirfield to be governess in the home of Mrs. Blake of Blake Hill. Emily came back from Law Hill to take care of things at home. And she herself went as governess to the Sidgwicks at Stonegappe. Her experiences as a governess were for the most part shattering to Charlotte's nature. From the parsonage doorstep she had gone forth to school and employment a dreamer, her head

full of wishful thinking. When the dreams came in direct
contact and conflict with reality, she was filled with the aches
of doubt and frustration, and these in turn made a rebel of
her. She rebelled, first of all, against the attitude of employer
toward employee. She did not understand that such a tone of
social superiority was not directed against her personally,
that it was the conventional one of the period. She felt humiliated, and she struck back. Her opinion of the Sidgwicks
is succinctly expressed in a letter to Emily:

I have striven hard to be pleased with my new situation. The country, the house, and the grounds are, as I
have said, divine. But, alack-a-day! there is such a thing
as seeing all beautiful around you—and not having a free
moment or a free thought left to enjoy them in. The children are constantly with me, and more riotous, perverse,
unmanageable cubs never grew. As for correcting them,
I soon quickly found that was entirely out of the question: they are to do as they like. A complaint to Mrs. Sidgwick brings only black looks upon oneself, and unjust,
partial excuses to screen the children. I have tried that
plan once. It succeeded so notably that I shall try it no
more. I now begin to find that she does not intend to
know me, that she cares nothing in the world about me
except to contrive how the greatest possible quantity of
labour may be squeezed out of me, and to that end she
overwhelms me with oceans of needlework, yards of cam-
bric to hem, muslin night-caps to make, and, above all
things, dolls to dress. I do not think she likes me at all,
because I can't help being shy in such an entirely novel
scene, surrounded as I have hitherto been by strange and
constantly changing faces. I see now more clearly than I
have ever done before that a private governess has no
existence, is not considered as a living and rational being

except as connected with the wearisome duties she has to fulfil. While she is teaching the children, working for them, it is all right. If she steals a moment for herself she is a nuisance. Nevertheless, Mrs. Sidgwick is universally considered an amiable woman. Her manners are fussily affable. She talks a great deal, but as it seems to me not much to the purpose. Perhaps I may like her better after a while. At present I have no call to her. Mr. Sidgwick is, in my opinion, a hundred times better—less profession, less bustling condescension, but a far kinder heart. It is very seldom that he speaks to me, but when he does I always feel happier and more settled for some minutes after. He never asks me to wipe the children's smutty noses or tie their shoes or fetch their pinafores or set them a chair. One of the pleasantest afternoons I have spent here—indeed, the only one at all pleasant—was when Mr. Sidgwick walked out with his children, and I had orders to follow a little behind. As he strolled on through his fields, with his magnificent Newfoundland dog at his side, he looked very like what a frank, wealthy, Conservative gentleman ought to be. He spoke freely and unaffectedly to the people he met, and though he indulged his children and allowed them to tease himself far too much, he would not suffer them grossly to insult others.

And, a week later, she writes to Ellen Nussey:

I must not bother you too much with my sorrows, of which, I fear you have heard an exaggerated account. If you were near me, perhaps, I might be tempted to tell you all, to grow egotistical, and pour out the long history of a private governess's trials and crosses in her first situation. As it is, I will only ask you to imagine the miseries of a reserved wretch like me thrown at once into the

69

midst of a large family, proud as peacocks and wealthy as Jews, at a time when they were particularly gay, when the house was filled with company—all strangers: people whose faces I had never seen before. In this state I had a charge given of a set of horrid children, whom I was expected constantly to amuse, as well as instruct. I soon found that the constant demand on my stock of animal spirits reduced them to the lowest state of exhaustion; at times I felt—and, I suppose seemed—depressed. To my astonishment, I was taken to task on the subject by Mrs. Sidgwick, with a sternness of manner and a harshness of language scarcely credible. Like a fool, I cried bitterly. I could not help it; my spirits quite failed me at first. I thought I had done my best, strained every nerve to please her; and to be treated that way, merely because I was shy and sometimes melancholy, was too bad. At first I was for giving all up and going home. But after a little reflection, I determined to summon what energy I had, and to weather the storm. I said to myself, "I had never yet quitted a place without gaining a friend; adversity is a good school; the poor are born to labour, and the dependent to endure." I resolved to be patient, to command my feelings, and to take what came; the ordeal, I reflected, would not last many weeks, and I trusted it would do me good. I recollected the fable of the willow and the oak; I bent quietly and now I trust the storm is blowing over. Mrs. Sidgwick is generally considered an agreeable woman; so she is, I doubt not, in general society. Her health is sound, her animal spirits good, consequently she is cheerful in company. But oh! does this compensate for the absence of every fine feeling, of every gentle and delicate sentiment? She behaves more civilly to me now than she did at first, and the children are a little more manageable; but she does not know my character, and she does not wish to know it. I have never had five minutes conversation with her since I came, except when she was scolding me. I have no wish to be pitied except by yourself.

Charlotte had left the Sidgwicks, and little wonder, by the midsummer of 1839, but the experience, as Mr. Shorter says, "rankled for many a long day." "It is not necessary to assume any very serious inhumanity on the part of the Sidgwicks," he added. "Hers was hardly a temperament adapted for that docile part; and one thinks of the author of *Villette,* possessed of one of the most vigorous prose styles in our language, condemned to a perpetual manufacture of night-caps, with something like a shudder." But it is quite possible that Charlotte would not have become the great novelist she became unless she had cut her teeth on the rough edges of personal friction. The shrewd analyses of character growing out of her associations at Miss Wooler's, the Sidgwicks, the Whites (where she went for a short term after her service at the Sidgwicks), all contributed a quantity of grist to Charlotte's creative mill. Her relationship to others forced upon her a keen sense of *self,* giving her an aptitude for self-analysis that also added greatly to her genius. For instance, she wrote Ellen:

I have some qualities that make me very miserable, some feelings that you can have no participation in—that few, very few people in the world can at all understand. I don't pride myself on these peculiarities. I strive to conceal and suppress them as much as I can, but they burst out sometimes, and then those who see the explosion despise me, and I hate myself for days afterwards.... You have been very kind to me of late, and have spared me all those little sallies of ridicule, which, owing to my

71

miserable and wretched *touchiness of character*, used formerly to make me wince, as if I had been touched with a hot-iron; things that nobody else cares for enter my mind and rankle there like venom. I know these feelings are absurd, and therefore I try to hide them, but they only sting the deeper for concealment.

Rebellious and passionate, endowed with a blazing imagination and sensitive perceptions, Charlotte Brontë found it difficult to curb her headstrong nature, which had a tendency to become vindictive when too directly crossed.

It is always futile to speculate on what might have been if so-and-so had happened instead of such-and-such. Yet one cannot but suppose that Charlotte's life would have turned out quite differently had she married at the first opportunity. If she had married in 1839, she would have escaped much of the travail that beset her during the following years, and yet she would have had to sacrifice the very things that were to be her salvation. For all her unstable emotional make-up, Charlotte was calculating and wise when it came to her deep-rooted ambitions. Somewhere at the outer fringes of her consciousness she felt that one or another of the Brontës, perhaps Emily or Branwell, even possibly herself, was fated to make the name of Brontë a name to be conjured with. While love was one thing she craved, with a pure and exalted idea of its completeness, she did not intend to compromise either her love or her future by becoming just another poor curate's wife in order to have a roof over her head, or to escape being a spinster.

Charlotte's first proposal came from Ellen Nussey's brother, Henry Nussey, the curate at Bonnington. Mr. Nussey proposed by letter, as did her second suitor, Mr. Price, a young Irish clergyman, not long from Dublin University,

and who was also a curate of the neighborhood. This method
of communicating one's fondest hopes to the object of
one's affections seems to have been the custom of the day.
I suppose it was intended to give the young lady in question
an opportunity to marshal her thoughts and phrase acceptance or refusal in terms that would do both of them justice.
Certainly Charlotte took full advantage of the opening to
express herself with due consideration for Mr. Nussey, and
for his sentiments, at the same time making her own argument for the opposition quite effective. The letter she wrote
him bears quoting in full:

> My dear sir,— Before answering your letter I might
> have spent a long time in consideration of its subject;
> but as from the first moment of its reception and perusal
> I determined on what course to pursue, it seemed to me
> that delay was wholly unnecessary. You are aware that I
> have many reasons to feel grateful to your family, that
> I have peculiar reasons for affection towards one at least
> of your sisters, and also that I highly esteem yourself—
> do not therefore accuse me of wrong motives when I say
> that my answer to your proposal must be a *decided nega-
> tive.* In forming this decision, I trust I have listened to the
> dictates of conscience more than to those of inclination.
> I have no personal repugnance to the idea of a union with
> you, but I feel convinced that mine is not the sort of dis-
> position calculated to form the happiness of a man like
> you. It has always been my habit to study the characters
> of those amongst whom I chance to be thrown, and I
> think I know yours and can imagine what description of
> woman would suit you for a wife. The character should
> not be too marked, ardent, and original, her temper
> should be mild, her piety undoubted, her spirits even and
> cheerful, and her *personal attractions* sufficient to please

73

your eyes and gratify your just pride. As for me, you do not know me; I am not the serious, grave, cool-headed individual you suppose; you would think me romantic and eccentric; you would say I was satirical and severe. However, I scorn deceit, and I will never, for the sake of attaining the distinction of matrimony and escaping the stigma of an old maid, take a worthy man whom I am conscious I cannot render happy. Before I conclude, let me thank you warmly for your other proposal regarding the school near Bonnington. It is kind in you to take so much interest about me; but the fact is, I could not at present enter upon such a project because I have not the capital necessary to insure success. It is a pleasure to me to hear that you are so comfortably settled and that your health is so much improved. I trust God will continue His kindness towards you. Let me say also that I admire the good-sense and absence of flattery and cant which your letter displayed. Farewell. I shall always be glad to hear from you as a *friend*.

And to Ellen, who wrote asking whether she had received her brother's letter, she also wrote an explanation:

I have, about a week since. The contents, I confess, did a little surprise me, but I kept them to myself, and unless you had questioned me on the subject, I would never have adverted to it. Now, my dear Ellen, there were in this proposal some things which might have proved a strong temptation. I thought if I were to marry Henry Nussey, his sister could live with me, and how happy I should be. But again I asked myself two questions: Do I love him as much as a woman ought to love the man she marries? Am I the person best qualified to make him happy? Alas! Ellen, my conscience answered *no* to both these questions. I felt that though I esteemed, though I had a kindly leaning towards him, because he is an amiable and well-disposed man, yet I had not, and could not have, that intense attachment which would make me willing to die for him; and, if ever I marry, it must be in that light of adoration that I will regard my husband. Ten to one I shall never have the chance again; but *n'importe.* Moreover, I was aware that Henry knew so little of me he could hardly be conscious to whom he was writing. Why, it would startle him to see me in my natural home character; he would think I was a wild, romantic enthusiast indeed. I could not sit all day long making a grave face before my husband. I would laugh, and satirise, and say whatever came into my head first. And if he were a clever man, and loved me, the whole world weighed in the balance against his smallest wish should be light as air. Could I, knowing my mind to be such as that, conscientiously say that I would take a grave, quiet young man like Henry? No, it would have been deceiving him, and deception of that sort is beneath me.

The second proposal, from Mr. Price, Charlotte took lightly, as was only natural, since it came after a single call at the parsonage in which the young curate had accompanied his vicar on a visit to Mr. Brontë. And telling Ellen of the incident, she dismissed matrimony from her life once and for all!

A few days after, I got a letter, the nature of which puzzled me, it being in a hand I was not accustomed to see. Evidently it was neither from you nor Mary, my only correspondents. Having opened and read it it proved to be a declaration of attachment and proposal of marriage from the sapient young Irishman! I hope you are laughing heartily. This is not like one of my adventures, is it? It more nearly resembles Martha's. I am certainly doomed to be an old maid. Never mind. I made up my mind to that fate ever since I was twelve years old. Well! I thought, I have heard of love at first sight, but this beats all. I leave you to guess what my answer would be, convinced you will not do me the injustice of guessing wrong.

By 1841 there was little hope that Branwell would make a way for himself, or be anyone that his sisters could turn to for either moral or financial support. Charlotte insisted that he seek employment, and he did attempt a clerkship in the railway, a job which turned out to be a dismal failure. Poor Charlotte was at her wit's end to devise a plan whereby she and Emily and Anne could remain together and yet gain sufficient livelihood to keep body and soul together. She herself no longer wanted to work as a governess, and teaching, at least under such conditions as she had previously encountered, was also to be avoided if possible. Anne's health was no better, and Charlotte was constantly worried about her, particularly while Anne was enduring such drudgery and hardship at the Robinsons, where she had gone after two years with the Blakes at Mirfield. At this point it occurred to Charlotte that the three of them might open a school of their own; and Miss Wooler, who remained in close touch with Charlotte, and who had been considering retirement for some time, now offered to step down in her favor. Charlotte was coolly appreciative of the offer, in her detached way, but was not ready to accept it, apparently having other plans already formulated. "I am not going to Dewsbury Moor," she wrote Ellen, "as far as I can see at present. It was a decent proposal on Miss Wooler's part, and cancels all or most of her little foibles, in my estimation; but Dewsbury Moor is a poisoned place to me; besides I burn to go somewhere else. I think, Nell, I see a chance of getting to Brussels." If she was going to conduct a school of her own, one can only suppose she felt the need for further training in French, and possibly German. If she could raise the money necessary for taking over the school at Dewsbury Moor she could certainly raise a sufficient amount to go abroad, even take Emily along.

With the thought of going to Belgium we find Charlotte in a mood of delighted anticipation quite alien to her usual lack of hope. The idea had been suggested by Martha Taylor, Mary's sister, who was herself at school in Brussels. But now the question was, where to raise the money for the undertaking. Aunt Elizabeth had been ready to help financially in the acquisition of Miss Wooler's School. Could she be made to see that it was as important, possibly more important, to invest money in furthering her niece's education? She would *have* to be persuaded. Charlotte had her heart set on going abroad. She wrote Aunt Elizabeth, and the letter is a self-portrait of Charlotte as she was that day, September 29, 1841, when her hopes were at the crossroads of their fulfillment. Mr. Clement Shorter published the letter for the first time from the original, which was in possession of Charlotte's widower, Arthur Bell Nichols; I reproduce it here:

Dear Aunt,— I have heard nothing of Miss Wooler yet since I wrote to her intimating that I would accept the offer. I cannot conjecture the reason of this long silence, unless some unforeseen impediment has occurred in concluding the bargain. Meantime, a plan has been suggested and approved by Mr. and Mrs. White, and others, which I wish now to impart to you. My friends recommend me, if I desire to secure permanent success, to delay commencing the school for six months longer, and by all means to contrive, by hook or crook, to spend the intervening time in some school on the continent. They say schools in England are so numerous, competition so great, that without some such step towards superiority we shall probably have a very hard struggle, and may fail in the end. They say, moreover, that the loan of one hundred pounds, which you have been so kind as to offer us, will, perhaps, not be all required now, as Miss Wooler will lend us the furniture; and that, if the speculation is intended to be a good and successful one, half the sum, at least, ought to be laid out in the manner I have mentioned, thereby insuring a more speedy repayment both of interest and principal.

I would not go to France or to Paris. I would go to Brussels, in Belgium. The cost of the journey there, at the dearest rate of travelling, would be five pounds; living there is little more than half as dear as it is in England, and the facilities for education are equal or superior to any other place in Europe. In half a year, I could acquire a thorough familiarity with French. I could improve greatly in Italian, and even get a dash of German, *i. e.*, providing my health continued as good as it is now. Martha Taylor is now staying in Brussels, at a first-rate establishment there. I should not think of going to the Chateau de Knockleberg, where she is resident, as the terms are much too high; but if I wrote to her, she, with the assistance of Mrs. Jenkins, the wife of the British Consul, would be able to secure me a cheap and decent residence and respectable protection. I should have the opportunity of seeing her frequently, she would make me acquainted with the city; and, with the assistance of her cousins, I should probably in time be introduced to connections far more improving, polished, and cultivated, than any I have yet known.

There are advantages which would turn to vast account, when we actually commenced a school—and, if Emily could share them with me, only for a single half-year, we could take a footing in the world afterwards which we can never do now. I say Emily instead of Anne; for Anne might take her turn at some future period, if our school answered. I feel certain, while I am writing, that you will see the propriety of what I say; you always like to use your money to the best advantage; you are not fond of making shabby purchases; when you do confer a favor, it is often done in style; and depend upon it fifty pounds, or one hundred pounds, thus laid out, would be well employed. Of course, I know no other friend in the world to whom I could apply on this subject except yourself. I feel an absolute conviction that, if this advantage were allowed us, it would be the making of us for life. Papa will perhaps think it a wild and ambitious scheme; but who ever rose in the world without ambition? When he left Ireland to go to Cambridge University, he was as ambitious as I am now. I want us *all* to go on. I know we have talents, and I want them to be turned to account. I look to you, aunt, to help us. I think you will not refuse. I know, if you consent, it shall not be my fault if you ever repent your kindness. With love to all, and the hope that you are well,— Believe me, dear aunt, your affectionate niece.

Aunt Elizabeth generously granted the loan, and in February, 1842, Mr. Brontë accompanied Charlotte and Emily to Brussels, entering them in the Pensionnat Heger, in the rue d'Isabelle. The pensionnat was in the charge of Madame Heger, but her husband conducted the classes in literature, and taught Latin at the Royal Athenée, a boy's school nearby.

The six months at the Heger Pensionnat were the happiest

months of Charlotte's life. Her spirit rose to its brightest; her understanding of others developed to its fullest extent; she made friends widely. Among her closest friends were numbered Mrs. Jenkins, wife of the British Consul, Dr. Wheelwright and his two daughters, and of course Martha Taylor, who had inspired Charlotte to come to the pensionnat, being a pupil there herself. Dr. Wheelwright was in Brussels for his health, and his daughters were day students at the school. One of them, Letitia Wheelwright, became a lasting friend. Emily, unfortunately, held aloof from these outside pleasures and associations; in fact, Charlotte's friends were shocked at her lack of sociability. But Emily was homesick, besides which, she had come abroad to study and would not be diverted. Mr. Shorter says that both sisters went to Brussels to learn, and that "they *did* learn, with energy. But it was their first experience of foreign travel, and it came too late in life for them to enter into it with that breadth of mind, and tolerance of the customs of other lands, lacking which the Englishman abroad is always an offense."

Aunt Elizabeth died in October of 1842, and Charlotte and Emily hurriedly returned to Haworth. They found that Aunt Elizabeth's will, after distribution of all personal belongings, divided an estate of fifteen hundred pounds among her four nieces: Charlotte, Emily, and Anne Brontë, and Elizabeth Jane Kingston, the daughter of another sister. With this legacy, Charlotte and her sisters were to enjoy their first economic freedom. And it meant that Charlotte, only a few months later, returned as on wings to the Heger Pensionnat.

This second journey to Brussels has, as everyone knows, led to the wildest controversy. Mr. Shorter has preferred to say that it gave rise to "speculation, some of it not of the pleasantest kind," though he agrees with May Sinclair that it is ridiculous to assume that Charlotte was in love with M. Heger. Not even Charlotte's own words had been able to convince Mr. Shorter and Miss Sinclair: "I returned to Brussels after Aunt's death against my conscience, prompted by what then seemed an irresistible impulse. I was punished for my selfish folly by a total withdrawal, for more than two years, of happiness and peace of mind." To what else could this refer except to an attachment that drew her as a flame draws a moth, and for which she payed with a burning heart. We know that on returning to Haworth, in December of 1843, she entered a period of anguished sufferings, when longing and pride battled within. There were nights of sleeplessness and torture, days of hope for the letters that never came, long talks with Emily, her only confidante. Charlotte was, as Esther Chadwick says, "wrestling with the experience that caused her to leave Brussels for the last time." Yet, even as she wrestled with her conscience, she continued to write to M. Heger. M. Heger, meanwhile, carelessly disposed of her letters * in the waste-paper basket, from which they were surreptitiously rescued by Madame Heger and preserved in her jewel box. Had Charlotte not become a famous novelist her letters to M. Heger, as those to Ellen Nussey or Mary Taylor, would have been gone with the wind. But as it was, M. Heger's son, Paul, into whose hands the letters ultimately fell, preserved them as a national treasure, and finally presented them to the British Museum. They were published in the *London Times* of July 29, 1913.

No one at Haworth except Emily was aware that Charlotte had left at least a half of herself behind in Brussels, that she had been torn from someone she loved. But, as usual, she communicated her grief to Ellen:

* See Appendix.

81

I suffered much before I left Brussels. I think, however long I live, I shall not forget what the parting with M. Heger cost me. It grieved me so much to grieve him who had been so true, kind, and disinterested a friend.... I do not know whether you feel as I do, but there are times now when it appears to me as if all my ideas and feelings, except a few friendships and affections, are changed from what they used to be: something in me, which used to be enthusiasm, is tamed down and broken. I have fewer illusions; what I wish for now is active exertion—a stake in life. Haworth seems such a lonely, quiet spot, buried away from the world. I no longer regard myself as young—indeed, I shall soon be twenty-eight; and it seems as if I ought to be working and braving the rough realities of the world, as other people do. It is, however, my duty to restrain this feeling at present, and I will endeavor to do so.

The "active exertion" that was to win her "a stake in life" was actually just around the corner. Fate, having played havoc with her heart, was now to set her feet on the path of fame. In 1845 the fever of creative energy that had used to warm them as children was again to seize upon Charlotte, Emily, and Anne. The result was an explosion of genius unparalleled in literary annals. From Charlotte's pen came *The Professor*, from Emily's *Wuthering Heights*, and from Anne's *Agnes Grey*.

Charlotte's first novel, *The Professor*, was rejected by a number of the publishers, but it paved the way for the publication of *Jane Eyre*, which followed in rapid succession. Yet even with *Jane Eyre* in print it was some little time before there was any personal triumph of success. In the first place, the novel appeared under Charlotte's earlier pseudonym,

Currer Bell, used for the poetry. Even Ellen Nussey and Mary Taylor were unaware of their friend's authorship. Only Emily and Anne knew the truth. Branwell was to die without ever knowing. And it was not until the book was by way of being what we would today call a best seller, critics to the contrary, that Mr. Brontë was informed of his daughter's achievement. The conversation between father and daughter is given by Mrs. Gaskell in her biography:

When the demand for the work had assured success to *Jane Eyre*, her sisters urged Charlotte to tell their father of its publication. She accordingly went into his study one afternoon, after his early dinner, carrying a copy of the book, and two or three reviews, taking care to include an adverse notice.

She informed me that something like the following conversation took place between them. (I wrote down her words the day after I heard them, and I am pretty sure they are quite accurate.)

"Papa, I've written a book."

"Have you, my dear?"

"Yes; and I want you to read it."

"I am afraid it will try my eyes too much."

"But it is not in manuscript; it is printed."

"My dear! you've never thought of the expense it will be! It will be almost sure to be a loss, for how can you get a book sold? No one knows you or your name."

"But papa, I don't think it will be a loss; no more will you, if you will just let me read you a review or two, and tell you more about it."

So she sat down and read some of the reviews to her father; and then giving him a copy of *Jane Eyre* that she intended for him, she left him to read it. When he came in to tea, he said, "Girls, do you know Charlotte has been writing a book, and it is much better than likely?"

Charlotte began her third novel in the first flush of *Jane Eyre*'s success, but it was while she was writing *Shirley* that death again came on terrible wings and took three more of the Brontë family. It seems truly incredible that any one family could have been so singled out for both tragedy and immortality, the two extremes of our scale of human values. As fame flew in one window of the parsonage the souls of Branwell, Emily, and Anne left by another. Branwell's last two years had been so fraught with illness, despair, delusions and ravings, he had been so wasted and bitter, that death was almost welcome. Charlotte had ceased to be interested in what happened to him. She continued to pity him in a way, but her disappointment in him, and her aggravation over his follies and uselessness, far exceeded her sympathy with his suffering.

It was quite another matter when it came to the loss of Emily and Anne. Here agony of soul descended upon Charlotte, and it was only by a miracle of fortitude and spiritual strength that she rose to continue her appointed tasks. No more than three months after Branwell's death, Emily was prey to the tuberculosis that had in all probability been lying dormant in every Brontë child since the sad days when Maria and Elizabeth had been its victims. And Emily had no more than been laid in the crypt under the aisle of the church next door when Anne began to fail. In a desperate effort to save her, Charlotte took her to the sea at Scarborough. But it was too late. Anne was also gone before the spring of 1849 had passed. After her death Charlotte was close to collapse, and in order to recuperate, went to stay with a friend, a Mrs. Hudson, at Easton. And it was here, after a period of rest in pleasant and happy surroundings, that she went back to her writing, picking up *Shirley* where she had left off the year before. But the return to Haworth was inevitable; again she was swept down by the memories, by desuetude of spirit and searing grief. Her heroism in the face of adversity remained with her, for she wrote Ellen Nussey a letter of surpassing sadness, yet sustained with the will to survive:

I do not much like giving an account of myself. I like better to go out of myself, and talk of something more cheerful. My cold, wherever I got it, whether at Easton or elsewhere, is not vanished yet. It began in my head, then I had a sore throat, and then a sore chest, with a cough, but only a trifling cough, which I still have at times. The pain between my shoulders likewise amazed me much. Say nothing about it, for I confess I am much disposed to be nervous. This nervousness is a horrid phantom. I dare communicate no ailment to Papa; his anxiety harasses me inexpressibly.

My life is what I expected it to be. Sometimes when I wake in the morning, and know that Solitude, Remembrance, and Longing are to be almost my sole companions all day through—that at night I shall go to bed with them, that they will long keep me sleepless—that next morning I shall wake to them again,—sometimes, Nell, I have a heavy heart of it. But crushed I am not, yet; nor robbed of elasticity, nor of hope, nor quite of endeavour. I have some strength to fight the battle of life. I am aware, and can acknowledge, I have many comforts, many mercies. Still I can *get on*. But I do hope and pray, that never may you, or any one I love, be placed as I am. To sit in a lonely room—the clock ticking loud through a still house—and have opened before the mind's eye the

record of the last year, with its shocks, sufferings, losses—
is a trial. I write to you freely, because I believe you will
hear me with moderation—that you will not take alarm
or think me in any way worse off than I am.

*Shirley* was finished in September, 1849, and Mr. James
Taylor, of the editorial department of Smith, Elder, visited
Haworth to pick up the manuscript. His visit was to be the
beginning of another romance for Charlotte, again one-sided,
which led to several urgent proposals on the part of the per-
sistent Scotchman. If Mr. Taylor had not been sent to Bom-
bay to open a branch office for his firm, it is quite possible
that Charlotte might have one day surrendered, for, after
nine months of remembrance, Charlotte could say of him,
"This little Taylor is deficient neither in spirit nor sense." That
was high recommendation from Charlotte!

The publication of *Shirley* and the interest stirred by *Jane
Eyre* made Charlotte somewhat of a literary celebrity. She
was invited to London and was given a little social whirl,
becoming acquainted with the artistic life of the great
metropolis. She went up to town at least four times during
the next months, and was always the house guest of Mr.
George Smith, the head of Smith, Elder, and his mother, at
their houses on Gloucester Terrace, Bishop's Place, and West-
bourne Place, Hyde Park. It was in their home that Charlotte
first met Thackeray, whom she so greatly admired, having
said that he possessed a "Titan of a mind." And when she
discovered that Harriet Martineau, author of *Deerbrook,* was
the Smiths' nearby neighbor, she sent her a copy of *Shirley* and was invited to tea in consequence. The incident was
the beginning of a short friendship between them which
went on the rocks after Miss Martineau criticized *Shirley* too

severely. However, before the break, Charlotte was to visit Miss Martineau at Ambleside in the Lake District, and thereby have the opportunity of meeting Mrs. Thomas Arnold, widow of the famous headmaster of Rugby, and her son, Matthew Arnold. She was not well impressed by either. "Mrs. Arnold's manner," she wrote James Taylor, "on introduction disappointed me sensibly, as lacking that genuineness and simplicity one seemed to have a right to expect in the chosen life-companion of Dr. Arnold. On my remarking as much to Mrs. Gaskell and Sir J. K. Shuttleworth, I was told for my consolation that it was a 'conventional manner,' but that it vanished on closer acquaintance; fortunately this last assurance proved true. It is observable that Matthew Arnold, the eldest son, and author of the volume of poems to which you allude, inherits his mother's defect. Striking and prepossessing in appearance, his manner displeases from its seeming foppery. I own it caused me at first to regard him with regretful surprise; the shade of Dr. Arnold seemed to frown on his young representative."

Charlotte made another visit to the Lake Country when she went to stay a week with Sir James K. Shuttleworth and his wife. The Shuttleworths lived at Gawthorpe Hall, a fine mansion seven or eight miles across the moors from Haworth. They had been much impressed by Charlotte's novels, and had called at the parsonage to express their admiration. Their interest so pleased Mr. Brontë, who was partial to the attentions of society, that he urged Charlotte to accept their invitations, though she was most reluctant to be under obligation to them. The result was that she went to their summer home in Westmoreland, and it was on this occasion that she met Mrs. Gaskell for the first time. As we know, the meeting was to bear fruit to Charlotte's lasting advantage, since Mrs. Gaskell proved to be one of the best-informed and most painstaking biographers of the Brontë family.

Of Charlotte's visits to London, the most important took place in 1850. She was entertained by Thackeray, attended the opera, and sat for her portrait by George Richmond, R. A. George Smith arranged for the picture, and it is considered a splendid likeness. The artist attributed his success largely to an incident that took place during the sittings. When Charlotte arrived at the studio one afternoon he told her that had she come a little earlier she would have met the aged Duke of Wellington. Charlotte's face, he claimed, was so transformed by the mere mention of Wellington, particularly in the expression of the eyes, that he was able to capture the mood and quality that made the portrait so remarkable a likeness.

It was also concerning the 1850 interlude in London that a controversy has arisen. Did Charlotte secretly leave London at this time, and if she did, where did she go? With whom (was it George Smith?) and to see whom (was it M. Heger in Brussels?). She wrote a note to Letitia Wheelwright, who lived in London, that she expected to be out of town a few days, and would see her on her return. She wrote Ellen Nussey saying she had "business to transact," but said nothing about going out of London to transact it. And a letter to her father, written at the same time, refers neither to an absence from the Smiths, with whom she was staying, *nor* to any business to be done elsewhere. Mrs. George Smith said she was not aware that her son had gone to Brussels with Charlotte at any time whatever. But, according to Miss Chadwick, the business Charlotte had to tend to on the Continent derived from what appears to have been a plagiarism

Charlotte Brontë, 1816–55, by George Richmond. *Copyright, National Portrait Gallery, London.*

Emily Brontë, 1818–34. Painting by Patrick Brontë. *Copyright, National Portrait Gallery, London.*

of *Jane Eyre* by M. Eugène Sue in his story entitled "Kitty Bell, the Orphan." Miss Chadwick's opinion is that the story was actually written by Charlotte, a preliminary sketch of the early chapters of *Jane Eyre*, either when she was in Brussels in 1843, or later. In which case the Hegers may have had a copy in their possession, given them at the time, or sent to them, by Charlotte herself. Possibly it fell into the hands of Eugène Sue, who did little to alter it before presenting it under his own name. Mr. George Smith might have considered it necessary for Charlotte to threaten suit against M. Sue, hence the "power of attorney" for which Charlotte paid Mr. Smith a known fee. There are much doubt and confusion and conflicting evidence with regard to these missing days in Charlotte's life, yet the balance of opinion would lead one to feel that she *did* go to Paris or Brussels, or both, and that, though she may not have seen M. Heger, yet revisiting the old scenes affected her so poignantly that *Villette* literally poured itself from her reawakened heart.

In 1851 Charlotte made three journeys from home. She visited Mrs. Gaskell in Manchester, accompanied the Smiths to Scotland, and was once more in London for some little time. During the London visit she heard Thackeray lecture, and was greatly impressed with his simple and easy manner of delivery. She saw Mme. Rachel act, and was "transfixed with wonder," though repelled by "the tremendous force with which she expresses the very worst passions in their strongest essence." In a letter to her father dated June 26, 1851, she gave an account of her days which is indicative of a certain confidence existing between father and daughter. Also, in the mere fact that it includes "Mr. Nichols" among the few to whom she sent her best regards, it presaged the friendship which was to lead to Charlotte's marriage.

Dear Papa,— I have not yet been able to get away from London, but if all be well I shall go to-morrow, stay two days with Mrs. Gaskell at Manchester, and return home on Monday 30th *without fail.* During this week or ten days I have seen many things, some of them very interesting, and have also been in much better health than I was during the first fortnight of my stay in London. Sir James and Lady Shuttleworth have really been very kind, and most scrupulously attentive. They desire their regards to you, and send all manner of civil messages. The Marquis of Westminster and the Earl of Ellemere each sent me an order to see their private collection of pictures, which I enjoyed very much. Mr. Rogers, the patriarch-poet, now eighty-seven years old, invited me to breakfast with him. His breakfasts, you must understand, are celebrated throughout Europe for their peculiar refinement and taste. He never admits at that meal more than four persons to his table: himself and three guests. The morning I was there I met Lord Glenelg and Mrs. Davenport, a relation of Lady Shuttleworth's, and a very beautiful and fashionable woman. The visit was very interesting; I was glad that I had paid it after it was over. An attention that pleased and surprised me more than I think than any other was the circumstance of Sir David Brewster, who is one of the first scientific men of his day, coming to take me over the Crystal Palace and pointing out and explaining the most remarkable curiosities. You will know, dear papa, that I do not mention these things to boast of them, but merely because I think they will give you pleasure. Nobody, I find, thinks the worse of me for avoiding publicity and declining to go to large parties, and everybody seems truly courteous and respectful, a mode of behaviour which makes me grateful, as it ought to do. Good-bye till Monday. Give my best regards to Mr. Nichols, Tabby, and Martha, and— Believe me, your affectionate daughter.

The following year, 1852, seems to have been another sad and trying one for Charlotte. Grief and loneliness swept back upon her, possibly because she was not well, but also because she was engaged in writing *Villette,* a book that brought back every poignant memory to stab her heart, particularly those with Brussels. Also she felt obligated to make a pilgrimage to Scarborough to see that the stone over Anne's grave was properly refaced and relettered. But she wrote constantly throughout the summer and fall, and when *Villette* was finished in November, she wrote George Smith, "You will see that *Villette* touches on no matter of public interest. I cannot write books handling topics of the day; it is of no use trying. Nor can I write a book for its moral. Nor can I make up a philanthropic scheme, though I honour philanthropy." This she said despite her stated theory that "a work of fiction ought to be a work of creation; that the *real* should be sparingly introduced in the pages dedicated to the ideal."

Meanwhile, another curate had fallen in love with Charlotte, and this time she made up her mind to marry, love or no love. Arthur Bell Nichols, Mr. Brontë's curate, had long nursed his feelings for Charlotte in secret, but the day came when he had to speak. Mr. Nichols was a good but unimaginative man, conscientious in his duties, and of great help to Mr. Brontë. In spite of all this, Mr. Brontë never liked him. And there is no question as to how Charlotte felt. She respected him, seeing in this quiet, sturdy man a protection and refuge from the tragic memories and solitary thoughts, but she did not love him.

When Mr. Nichols went to Mr. Brontë with the request for his daughter's hand in marriage, Mr. Brontë flew into a violent temper and gave him to understand that he was most unacceptable as a son-in-law. The poor man left the parsonage utterly reduced, and standing by the gate bowed his head and wept, with Charlotte of course observing from the window. Mr. Nichols immediately resigned his curacy, and again broke down before the assembled congregation when giving Charlotte the sacrament for the last time before leaving. By this time Charlotte pitied him with all her heart, and pity must have played a large part in her determination to marry him. After several scenes with her father, who continued to protest that Mr. Nichols was in no way her equal, she finally persuaded him to relent. Mr. Nichols returned to Haworth as curate and they were married June 29, 1854. But the night before the wedding, when Charlotte went to her father's study to bid him good night, he informed her that he did not intend to be present at the ceremony next morning. Charlotte was not only deeply hurt and humiliated, but there was the vital question of who was to give her away, particularly at such short notice. She discussed the question with Miss Wooler and Ellen Nussey, who had already arrived, and after consulting the Bible they discovered that the service could be performed by a woman. So it was Miss Wooler who stood up with Charlotte, and not her own father, rector of the church where she was married.

Mr. Nichols took his bride to Ireland on their honeymoon. They visited relatives and friends, and made tours of Killarney, Klengariff, Tarbert, Tralae, Cork, and Charlotte was truly enchanted with the Irish scenery.

Back at Haworth, Charlotte's husband took over many of the parish duties, greatly relieving Mr. Brontë; and now, as wife and mistress of the parsonage, Charlotte found her days full of pleasant activities. It is told that on one occasion she played hostess to some five hundred of the parishioners: scholars, teachers, churchringers, and singers. But Charlotte's health, as we know, was not sturdy, and once again we find death lurking on the moors, always eager to find a fresh victim in the Brontë household.

Late in the fall of 1854, Charlotte took a long walk over the moors, against her better judgment, but urged on by a sense of duty, not wishing to appear unwilling or too frail to accompany her husband. But rain came on, and by the time she reached home she was chilled to the bone and deeply exhausted. It is quite possible that she was already with child, which would have made the illness that followed more acute. For shortly after we have Mrs. Gaskell reporting that she "was attacked by new sensations of perpetual nausea, and an ever-recurring faintness." She became so weak and ill that she was unable to retain the smallest amount of food, and her death, on March 31, 1855, was due, as Mr. Shorter has said, "to an illness incidental to childbirth."

Just before the end, in a moment of lucidity, she realized that her husband was praying beside her, and looking on his face worn with grief, she whispered, "Oh, I am not going to die, am I? He will not separate us, we have been so happy."

*Chapter* XI  EMILY

*"The earth that wakes one human heart to feeling
Can centre both the worlds of Heaven and Hell."*
E. BRONTË

E MILY," wrote Charles Morgan, "had two
lives. It was the essence of her genius that they were distinct.
One, the superficial life, the life of the daughter at the parsonage, which she is commonly praised for having led with
dutiful heroism, was not in her eyes heroic. It was the activity
in the midst of which she learned how to feed upon the spirit
within her." *

The child who romped over the Haworth moors, whose
reticence and withdrawal kept her apart from schoolmates,
and whose domestic labors in the parsonage fell like a curtain between the two worlds of her nature, turned out, by
virtue of a few poems and a strange puzzling novel, to have
been a pagan, a mystic, and a passionate woman. Biographical data, of a strictly circumstantial variety, is conspicu-
ously lacking in Emily's case. Yet of the Brontë sisters, it is
Emily with whom the critics and biographers have been
most concerned, particularly as regards her romantic attach-
ments, whatever those may have been. Here the controversy
over Emily becomes passionate. Was there a man, or men,
in Emily's life? And here we cannot but be reminded of
similar questions respecting another Emily, the Nun of Am-
herst. Speculation about the men who influenced Emily
Brontë involves one to three. Virginia Moore says there was

* From *The Great Victorians* by H. J. Massingham

94

a Louis Parensell, whom Emily met at Miss Patchet's School at Law Hill. The name was found on the manuscript of one of the poems written there, but the handwriting is supposed to be Charlotte's. What that tends to prove, one wouldn't know exactly. But Roamer Wilson, in order to confirm Mr. Parensell, groups a number of poems written at Law Hill under the title, *Poems of Guilt*. Then there is the rather subtle, if tenuous, case that Miss Chadwick makes out for Emily's affections being directed, together with her sister's, toward M. Heger of Brussels. M. Heger was, according to Miss Chadwick, "the first man to approach Emily Brontë's ideal," and she gives us a poem, written by Emily on May 17, 1842, "which helps to prove she had had a vision of perfect love in Brussels." Again may we say "yes, possibly." But the third alternative is more farfetched than either of these. The third is Branwell. Of course it can be fully admitted that there was a particular bond of sympathy and understanding between brother and sister. And it is perfectly true that when Charlotte and Anne became thoroughly exasperated with Branwell's behavior, realizing that he had progressed too far along the road to perdition ever to be reclaimed, Emily stood by. It was Emily who sat waiting night after night until Branwell returned from the tavern, often in a mood no woman likes to reckon with. It was Emily who saved Branwell with her own hands from the burning bed he had inadvertently, in a drunken stupor, set afire. But neither is it in the least necessary to accept Miss Kinsley's evidence, set forth in her shrewd but too shrewd book, *Pattern of Genius,* in which she attempts to prove the incestuous relationship by using their own written words from novel and poem as witness against them. "It was an awful and inexplicable communion," Miss Kinsley claims, "never to be explained and never to be wholly broken, a communion in the fourth dimension which existed between them as long as they lived." It is far better, I think, to accept Charles Morgan's sane and sensible comment on the subject: *

Let us, then, examine the works without seeking to prove in them either that Emily was in love with her brother or with any other man, or that she was incapable of bodily desire. It is unnecessary to proceed to either of these extremes, for the poems do not require them, and, though the closeness of Emily's later association with Branwell is deeply relevant to the authorship of *Wuthering Heights,* there is no just cause for assuming or suspecting that her love for him, if she loved him, was abnormal, except in the sense in which all emotional states were, by intensification and a disease of secrecy, made abnormal within the walls of Haworth. It is true that Charlotte's behavior to Branwell, her envenomed exclusion of him from her life during the period in which *Wuthering Heights* was being written, is not fully accounted for either by his pleasures of the inn or by the suggestion that, having been herself denied in her passion, she was made morally indignant and resentful by her brother's disgrace at Thorpe Green. Charlotte had many faults, but she was not a petty, spiteful spinster: there must have been better reasons than these for the long continuance of her hatred. It is true, also, that she displayed an extraordinary eagerness to obliterate all traces of her sister's private life, and that there is a hint of baffled terror in her reticences when she writes of Emily. On these and other indications it might be possible to build up a theory that the relationship of Branwell and Emily was one that displeased Charlotte, and that she

* From *The Great Victorians* by H. J. Massingham.

wished to conceal the nature of it. But the evidence is all conjectural and reacts against itself. We shall be wise to put this theory out of mind, and to proceed, for lack of available proof, on the assumption that it is altogether unfounded.

Whatever the exact explanation of the passionate spirit of Emily Brontë, biographers and commentators alike agree that she burned with an insatiable *hunger*. But what did she hunger *for*? Again it is common agreement that, whatever it was, it was beyond the reach of mortal flesh. The poetry and the novel blaze with the symbols of love and liberty, personal needs with universal significance. Charles Morgan believes that during her adolescent years Emily Brontë tasted the ecstasy of an exalted experience, and spent the rest of her days attempting to recapture it. She sought to possess the Absolute, and failing that would not be assuaged. And it is out of the abstraction of Emily's ideal that Roma Wilson has created her theory of a Demon Lover. Certainly some such demon pursued Catherine and Heathcliff in *Wuthering Heights*. In spite of Emily's outward calm, her stoical endurance, and stubborn, reserved disposition, she carried a tortured spirit within. Her real life existed only in her poetry. She cared nothing for fame or appreciation. She wrote to release the moods, the thoughts, that she could not wholly contain in her fragile body. She was a mystic, as we have said. Emily Brontë and William Blake were alike in one respect—they were unconcerned with individual salvation, but sought to bring mankind into harmony with the will and purpose of the Creator. To them human love and liberty are the roots we throw down, ever more firmly, into the universal mind, into "a mutual immortality," as she expressed it in the closing lines of "I See Around Me Tombstones Grey":

97

We all, in life's departing shine,
Our last dear longings blend with thine;
And struggle still and strive to trace
With clouded gaze, thy darling face.
We would not leave our native home
For *any* world beyond the Tomb.
No—rather on thy kindly breast
Let us be laid in lasting rest;
Or waken but to share with thee
A mutual immortality.

For all source of knowledge, Emily drew upon her own comprehending spirit. Miss Sinclair says, "There was in the great genius of Emily Brontë a dark unconscious instinct of primitive nature-worship. That was where she was so poised and so complete, where she touches earth and heaven, and is at once intoxicated with the splendor of the passion for living. It is what holds her spirit in security and her heart in peace.... And this woman, destitute, so far as can be known, of all metaphysical knowledge, reared in the narrowest and least metaphysical of creeds, did yet contrive to express in one poem... all the hunger and thirst after the 'Absolute' that ever moved a human soul, all the bewilderment and agony inflicted by the unintelligible spectacle of existence, the intolerable triumph of evil over good, and did conceive an image and a vision of the transcendent reality that holds, as in a crystal, all the philosophies that are worthy of the name." *

* Introduction by May Sinclair from *The Tenant of Wildfield Hall* and *Agnes Grey* by Anne Brontë, Everyman's Library, E. P. Dutton & Co. Inc., N. Y. Introduction by May Sinclair from *Jane Eyre* by Charlotte Brontë. Everyman's Library, E. P. Dutton & Co. Inc., N. Y. By permission J. M. Dent & Sons Ltd., London, and E. P. Dutton & Co. Inc., New York.

## "The Philosopher"

"Enough of Thought, Philosopher;
Too long hast thou been dreaming
Unenlightened, in this chamber drear
While summer's sun is beaming—
Space-sweeping soul, what sad refrain
Concludes thy musings once again?

"O for the time when I shall sleep
Without identity,
And never care how rain may steep
Or snow may cover me!

"No promised Heaven, these wild Desires
Could all or half fulfil;
No threatened Hell, with quenchless fires,
Subdue this quenchless will!"

—So said I, and still say the same;
—Still to my Death will say—
Three Gods within this little frame
Are warring night and day.

Heaven could not hold them all, and yet
They all are held in me
And must be mine till I forget
My present entity.

O for the time when in my breast
Their struggles will be o'er;
O for the day when I shall rest,
And never suffer more;

"I saw a Spirit standing, Man,
Where thou dost stand—an hour ago;
And round his feet, three rivers ran
Of equal depth and equal flow—

"A golden stream, and one like blood,
And one like Sapphire, seemed to be,
But where they joined their triple flood
It tumbled in an inky sea.

"The Spirit bent his dazzling gaze
Down on that Ocean's gloomy night,
Then—kindling all with sudden blaze,
The glad deep sparkled wide and bright—
White as the sun; far, far more fair
Than the divided sources were!"

—And even for that Spirit, Seer,
I've watched and sought my lifetime long;
Sought Him in Heaven, Hell, Earth, Air,
An endless search—and always wrong!

Had I but seen His glorious eye
*Once* light the clouds that 'wilder me,
I ne'er had raised this coward cry
To cease to think and cease to be—

I ne'er had called oblivion blest,
Nor stretching eager hands to Death
Implored to change for lifeless rest
This sentient soul, this living breath.

O let me die, that power and will
Their cruel strife may close,
And vanquished Good, victorious Ill
Be lost in one repose.

This Absolute Emily yearned for, and sought with such passionate desire, has been called, by some, her Demon Lover, by others, her Angel Lover. Out of the search for sign or image of her love springs the ecstasy between captive flesh and liberated spirit:

### "The Visionary"

What I love shall come like visitant of air,
Safe in secret power from lurking human snare;
Who loves me, no word of mine shall e'er betray,
Though for faith unstained my life must forfeit pay.

Burn, then, little lamp; glimmer straight and clear—
Hush! a rustling wing stirs, methinks, the air:
He for whom I wait, thus ever comes to me;
Strange Power! I trust thy might; trust thou my constancy.

The two stanzas above quoted have been taken, by editors, as a separate poem, from the "sequel" to the Gondal epic, one of Emily's longest and finest examples of sustained emotion. The entire poem bears the title, as in the manner of so many of the Gondal poems, *Julian M. and A. G. Rochelle.* Miss Sinclair says that this poem is constantly reminding her of "one of the most marvelous poems of Divine Love, 'En Una Noche Escura,' by St. John of the Cross." In the following stanzas the lady addresses Lord Julian:

"I cannot wonder now at aught the world will do,
  And insult and contempt I lightly brook from you,
  Since those, who vowed away their souls to win my love,
  Around this living grave like utter strangers move!

"Nor has one voice been raised to plead that I might die,
Not buried under earth but in the open sky;
By ball or speedy knife or headsman's skilful blow—
A quick and welcome pang instead of lingering woe!

"Yet, tell them, Julian, all, I am not doomed to wear
Year after year in gloom and desolate despair;
A messenger of Hope comes every night to me,
And offers, for short life, eternal liberty.

"He comes with western winds, with evening's wandering
    airs,
With that clear dusk of heaven that brings the thickest stars;
Winds take a pensive tone, and stars a tender fire,
And visions rise and change which kill me with desire—

"Desire for nothing known in my maturer years
When joy grew mad with awe at counting future tears;
When, if my spirit's sky was full of flashes warm,
I knew not whence they came, from sun or thunderstorm;

"But first a hush of peace, a soundless calm descends;
The struggle of distress and fierce impatience ends;
Mute music soothes my breast—unuttered harmony
That I could never dream till earth was lost to me.

"Then dawns the Invisible, the Unseen its truth reveals;
My outward sense is gone, my inward essence feels —
Its wings are almost free, its home, its harbour found;
Measuring the gulf it stoops and dares the final bound!

"Oh, dreadful is the check—intense the agony
When the ear begins to hear and the eye begins to see;
When the pulse begins to throb, the brain to think again,
The soul to feel the flesh and the flesh to feel the chain!

"Yet I would lose no sting, would wish no torture less;
    The more that anguish racks the earlier it will bless;
    And robed in fires of Hell, or bright with heavenly shine,
    If it but herald Death, the vision is divine."


"The soul to feel the flesh and the flesh to feel the chain!"
It was this bondage, the struggle and agony it meant, that
kept Emily on a rack of torture. She pursued the vision with
reverent devotion until it bathed her soul in the reflected
radiance of truth. The very essence of that radiance is what
she poured into one of the most familiar of her poems, "No
Coward Soul Is Mine":

> No coward soul is mine,
> No trembler in the world's storm-troubled sphere:
> I see Heaven's glories shine,
> And Faith shines equal arming me from Fear.
>
> O God within my breast
> Almighty ever-present Deity
> Life, that in me hast rest
> As I Undying Life, have power in Thee
>
> Vain are the thousand creeds
> That move men's hearts: unutterably vain;
> Worthless as withered weeds,
> Or idlest froth amid the boundless main,
>
> To waken doubt in me
> Holding so fast by Thine infinity;
> So surely anchored on
> The steadfast rock of Immortality

With wide-embracing love
Thy spirit animates eternal years
Pervades and broods above,
Changes, sustains, dissolves, creates and rears.

Though Earth and moon were gone,
The suns and universes ceased to be,
And Thou wert left alone
Every Existence would exist in Thee

There is not room for Death,
Nor atom that his might could render void:
Thou—Thou art Being and Breath
And what Thou art may never be destroyed.

Emily's love of nature, her sense of being one with the diurnal turn of the earth, of being a living part of the moor and its mists and winds, sunsets and sunrises, moods of grief and joy, give her poetry universal significance. It also explains why Emily was torn asunder when she was away from Haworth. It explains the fierce nostalgia that weakened even her body when she was cut off from the sweet harmony of life on the barren, heather-blue hills. Emily Brontë deprived of her beloved countryside was as Samson shorn of his locks. A poem that expresses the homesickness and longing that swept over her in alien climes is one she wrote either at Miss Patchet's School at Law Hill, in 1838, which is the date Mr. Hatfield claims for it, or during the desolate months in Brussels:

"A Little While, A Little While"

A little while, a little while,
The noisy crowd are barred away;
And I can sing and I can smile
A little while I've holyday!

Where wilt thou go, my harassed heart?
Full many a land invites thee now;
And places near and far apart
Have rest for thee, my weary brow.

There is a spot 'mid barren hills
Where winter howls and driving rain,
But if the dreary tempest chills
There is a light that warms again.

The house is old, the trees are bare
The moonless bends the misty dome
But what on earth is half so dear,
So longed for as the hearth of home?

The mute bird sitting on the stone,
The dank moss dripping from the wall,
The garden-walk with weeds o'ergrown,
I love them—how I love them all!

Shall I go there? or shall I seek
Another clime, another sky,
Where tongues familiar music speak
In accents dear to memory?

Yes, as I mused, the naked room,
The flickering firelight died away
And from the midst of cheerless gloom
I passed to bright, unclouded day—

A little and a lone green lane
That opened on a common wide;
A distant, dreamy, dim blue chain
Of mountains circling every side;

A heaven so clear, an earth so calm,
So sweet, so soft, so hushed an air
And, deepening still the dream-like charm,
With moor-sheep feeding everywhere—

Uncounted hours have been spent by students and critics alike in the attempt fully to recover, transcribe, arrange chronologically, and adjudicate the poetry of Emily Brontë. It was natural that all Emily's manuscripts, after her death, should have fallen into the hands of Charlotte, and later into those of Arthur Bell Nichols, Charlotte's widower. Mr. Nichols made an attempt to transcribe them, which was possibly a serious mistake, since he has been found guilty of many errors; and these might indicate others never checked for lack of the original manuscripts concerned. Mr. Clement Shorter, for instance, in editing the first collection of the poems that bear any claim to being definitive, repeats many of the errors for which Charlotte and Mr. Nichols are responsible. It is to Miss Fannie Ratchford that credit is due for her patient and perceptive work, her collations and transcriptions made directly from the texts of the scattered manuscripts, which laid the groundwork for the complete volume of the poems, edited by Mr. C. W. Hatfield and published in 1941. This volume gives the world at last, after nearly a century of groping research, Emily Brontë's full stature as a poet. There has been altogether too much attempt to extract biographical data from poetry that deserves to be treated as literature. There has always been someone hunting the key to Emily in her written words, since the facts of her life are so few and far between. But it is an unremunerative task the student has set himself, particularly since, in Emily's case, her life was entirely in the spirit, and had so little direct relation to reality. Whereas, if the reader, whether scholar or poet, would allow himself to be led into the spirit with her, to taste its joy and pain, a classification of the men in Emily's life would seem a kind of sacrilege. Emily's reality was not in this world. And, as Charles Morgan has so well said, "to one who had known this reality all other failure was less than the failure to recapture it, and over such a one the world had no power. Death appeared to her, in one aspect, as an end of the blissful torture she would not have lessened; in another aspect, as a possible reversal of her failures—an opportunity to be 'really in and with' the supreme familiar spirit. She did not know whether to dread death as a cessation or to desire it as an opportunity. She did not know whence her familiar spirit came, from heaven or from hell; she did not know whether, in the Christian view, her blisses were evil or good; she was not certain that, in going from this world, she might take her ecstasy with her."

One cannot but wonder how much this doubt and desire explains Emily's own death, which took place three months after Branwell's. From the day of his death she never set foot outside the parsonage. In October (Branwell had died in late September), she contracted a severe cold and developed a stubborn cough. Charlotte was deeply concerned, and in writing to Ellen expressed her anxiety: "I fear she has a pain in the chest, and I sometimes catch a shortness in her breathing, when she has moved at all quickly. She looks very, very thin and pale. Her reserved nature occasions me great unhappiness of mind. It is useless to question her—you get no answers. It is still more useless to recommend remedies—they are never adopted."

The agony persisted for two more months. Day after day Emily insisted on going about her household tasks. She refused to take medicine or see a doctor. Charlotte and Anne stood by in helpless anguish. Once, in desperation, Charlotte sent for a doctor, but when he came Emily refused to see him. She would not allow her sisters to refer to her condition. She grew steadily worse. She had often claimed she had no fear of death. Was she trying to prove it? Was she inwardly exultant that she would soon have the opportunity to taste the ecstasy of her reunion with the spirit? As Emily said when she was only twenty-two:

> Riches I hold in light esteem
> And love I laugh to scorn
> And lust of Fame was but a dream
> That vanished with the morn—
>
> And if I pray, the only prayer
> That moves my lips for me
> Is—"Leave the heart that now I bear
> And give me liberty."
>
> Yes, as my swift days near their goal
> 'Tis all that I implore—
> Through life and death, a chainless soul
> With courage to endure! *

On Tuesday, the nineteenth of December, Emily came downstairs and went about the usual household chores. By noon she was so weak she was unable to speak above a whisper. She sat by the open grate trying to comb her hair, but her hand was too feeble to hold the comb and it fell to the hearthstone. Charlotte went out on the moor to find "a linger-

* Above poems reprinted from *The Complete Poems of Emily Jane Brontë*, edited by C. W. Hatfield. Copyright 1941 by Columbia University Press.

ing spray of heather" with which to cheer her sister, but Emily was already beyond recognizing external objects. They moved her to a couch. She opened her eyes then, and whispered to Charlotte, "If you will send for a doctor, I will see him now." But when she closed her eyes again it was for the last time. There had died, that bleak December day, 1848, in the lonely parsonage of Haworth, the spirit that had bewitched it.

Emily's dog, Keeper, followed the coffin across the churchyard, into the church, and up the aisle; and when she was laid beneath the stone floor he returned to the parsonage, and lay down across the threshold of her room, refusing to be consoled.

*Chapter* XII   BRANWELL

I<small>T</small> IS probable," writes Esther Alice Chadwick, "that no character in literature has been made to suffer more for supposed misdeeds than Branwell Brontë. Whatever was wrong in the Brontë household, or the Brontë novels, has been generally attributed to Branwell, but he has been more sinned against than sinning." Of the women who have expressed themselves with regard to Branwell, Miss Chadwick is the most charitable, for most of them have treated him with considerable severity, fully sympathizing with his three sisters. The men on the other hand, including Francis Grundy and Francis Leyland, have been far more tolerant. They no doubt understood him better, judging by men's standards in a man's world.

We ask ourselves, was Branwell Brontë a genius without the will to express it? Yet true genius does not lack the will, labor being the essence of will. Branwell did not labor. Therefore was the idea of his inherent genius a family illusion, born in the hearts of his adoring sisters and a doting father, in whose eyes he could do no wrong, so that when he disappointed them the consciousness of failure was a boomerang that destroyed him? "He was half poet," says Edith Kinsley, "when he was not a maniac; he might have been a prophet had he not become a profligate. He had an electric temper which emitted ominous sparks, which his father said

110

was 'spirit,' and must not be curbed." An only son, spoiled by a too-indulgent yet indifferent father, idolized by three temperamental sisters, restrained from all association with boys of his own age who might have succeeded in beating his wayward nature to its knees, Branwell was more or less doomed to go on the rocks. Given a chance, psychiatry would only have predicted the worst!

Branwell was born at Thornton in 1817. When the family moved to Haworth he was three years old, and during the succeeding years, his education was what he had received at home; outside associations were frowned upon, and he was regarded as a priceless jewel which would one day shine for the honor and glory of the Brontë name. How this was to be accomplished seems to have been left to fate, since in all the records of the Brontë family there is none to indicate that Branwell was to get even a university degree. When one considers in what high esteem a degree was held, and what travail Mr. Brontë endured to win the honor himself, it is difficult to understand the omission in Branwell's case. Aunt Elizabeth would assuredly have seen the wisdom of giving her nephew such a start in life. Here was an only son, and many dependents. Yet the "career" finally decided upon for Branwell was that of an artist; and what career is less lucrative unless the artist has more than his share of ambition, concentration, and genius. Branwell, his family to the contrary, had none of these in marked degree. All the children showed an inclination to drawing, Branwell as well as his sisters. But it was for Branwell that Mr. Brontë engaged a drawing teacher. And it was Branwell, at the age of eighteen, who was sent up to London to study at the Royal Academy.

**111**

The money advanced for the academy was quickly lost in the gambling that had already become Branwell's weakness, and he was soon back in Haworth without a penny to his name. Mr. Brontë even refused to pay the debts his son had incurred. However, since it was clearly impossible to allow Branwell to become the ne'er-do-well of Haworth village, as he was apparently quite willing to do, having joined a convivial club, the "Lodge of the Three Graces," meeting at the Black Bull Tavern, it was decided that he should set up a studio in Bradford. There was the hope that through friends he might receive portrait commissions. But it was not to be. As Miss Kinsley says, "at the foot of his studio stairs was a public house, *The George,* where a group of artists consorted . . . to chat, eat, and get rid of the evening damp with a few cheerful drinks. Branwell, as before at *The Black Bull Tavern,* now found himself secure of attention at *The George* in the role of public entertainer. On the other hand, his ideas and his work were indifferently regarded. Therefore, he sought *The George* only as he had sought *The Bull,* for specious consolation to his vanity."

The Bradford studio experiment having thus failed miserably, Branwell next took a position as clerk in charge of the Sowerby Bridge station of the Leeds and Manchester Railway. After a year at Sowerby Bridge he was transferred to the station at Luddenden Foot; but here an act of negligence caused his dismissal. Some years later, referring to this period in a letter to Francis Grundy, he wrote, "My conduct there, lost as I was to all that I like or had hoped for, was marked by a malignant and yet cold debauchery, a determination to find how far mind could carry body, without both being chucked into hell—it was a nightmare."

"Lost as I was to all that I like or had hoped for!" What a

Anne Brontë. Painted by her sister, Charlotte, June 17, 1834. This is the only known portrait of Anne in existence. *Photograph by Walter Scott. Copyright, The Brontë Society.*

Patrick Branwell Brontë. The only known portrait. *Photograph by Walter Scott. Copyright, The Brontë Society.*

death knell the words sound. One cannot but have a rending sympathy for Branwell, whose life went so terribly askew, and by no means entirely due to his own shortcomings. It becomes obvious, as we follow Branwell down the rapid decline of his youth, that he was cut out to be more scholar than artist. Almost his only claim to literary ability, for instance, over and above the famous Knave of Hearts epistle, which immortalizes the name of the church sexton, John Brown, rests in his translations of Horace. Before taking the job with the Leeds Railway, he had sent a few of these translations to Hartley Coleridge, with a letter from which I take the following excerpt:

> Since my childhood, I have been wont to devote the hours I could spare from other and very different employments to efforts at literary composition, always keeping the results to myself, nor have they in more than two or three instances been seen by any other. But I am about to enter active life, and prudence tells me not to waste the time which must make my independence; yet, sir, I like writing too well to fling aside the practice of it without an effort to ascertain whether I could turn it to account, not in *wholly* maintaining myself, but in *aiding* my maintenance, for I do not sigh after fame, and am not ignorant of the folly of the fate of those who, without ability, would depend for their lives upon their pens; but I seek to know, and venture, though with shame, to ask from one whose word I must respect: whether, by periodical or other writing, I could please myself with writing, and make it subservient to living.

Apparently Hartley Coleridge was sufficiently interested to send for him, and Branwell spent a day with Coleridge at Ambleside a few weeks later. How much praise or advice

113

he received on this occasion is not clear, but it was apparently sufficient to encourage Branwell to pursue the subject:

I have, I fear most negligently, and amid other very different employments—striven to Translate two books, the first of which I have presumed to send you. And will you, sir, stretch your past kindness by telling me whether I should amend and pursue the work or let it rest in peace.

Great corrections I feel it wants, but till I feel that the work might benefit me, I have no heart to make them; yet if your judgment prove in any way favourable, I will re-write the whole, without sparing labour to reach perfection.

I dared not have attempted Horace but that I saw the utter worthlessness of all former translations, and thought that a better one, by whomsoever executed, might meet with some little encouragement. I long to clear up my doubts by the judgment of one whose opinion I should revere, and—but I suppose I am dreaming—one to whom I should be proud indeed to inscribe anything of mine which any publisher would look at, unless, as is likely enough, the work would disgrace the name as much as the name would honour the work.

Obviously Hartley Coleridge let the matter drop. Perhaps he was too busy to become involved in the hopes and future of a young unknown. Perhaps he honestly did not see that the work was in the least important. Whatever the cause, the result was that Branwell passed beyond hope and gave himself over to the demons of bitterness and waste. The translations of Horace were discovered, about twenty-five years ago, by the English poet, John Drinkwater, who edited and privately printed them. In a foreword Mr. Drinkwater states that the translations could hardly be improved: "There are passages of clear, lyrical beauty, and something of the style that comes from spiritual understanding, apart from merely formal knowledge of great models."

In December, 1842, Branwell again tried work, this time teaching. He went as tutor to the son of the Reverend Edmund Robinson at Thorpe Green. Anne, as we have seen, was governess in the same household. Once more fate dealt Branwell a cruel blow. The Robinson household was not the place for a young man of Branwell's egotism and attitude of mind. Mr. Robinson was ill and not expected to live; Mrs. Robinson, young, vivacious, and extremely sophisticated, was not averse to carrying on a flirtation to pass the time of day with a brilliant young man, charming in manner, eloquent in speech, and attractive to look upon. He appealed to her fancy and her vanity. She was looking for amusement, but Branwell fell madly in love. She encouraged him without reciprocation, or at least without sincerity.

Mr. Robinson could hardly be said to have savored the situation, which was all too apparent to both himself and Anne, and proceeded to dismiss Branwell in peremptory fashion. So again Branwell returned to Haworth under a cloud, and took up his familiar routine: drinking at The Black Bull Tavern, and lolling about the parsonage where he was the cause of the greatest consternation and dismay. But until Mr. Robinson's death he appeared to believe that Mrs. Robinson, once a widow, would call him back. If Mrs. Robinson ever had the idea in mind, she quickly dismissed it when, soon after her husband's demise, she was courted by Lord Scott, and went up to London to marry that gentleman. Charlotte and Anne tried as long as possible to keep the news of Mrs. Robinson's "betrayal" from reaching Branwell, knowing what it would do to him under the circumstances.

And Charlotte, though fiercely critical of Branwell for his folly and stupidity in the whole matter, was equally incensed at the treatment Mrs. Robinson had accorded her brother. "I suppose the affair was conducted as such affairs usually are," she wrote. "Branwell offered Mrs. Robinson his youth and his talents, such as they were, in exchange for her position and money. Love did not enter into the account. She was older than he and, Anne says, not beautiful. The lady, having no chance at the moment of making a better bargain, was inclined to come to terms with Branwell. Then Lord Scott, a flourishing and handsome nobleman, stepped in with a higher bid."

It was the outcome of this affair that lit the fuse of Branwell's mental illness. He had no further regard for anything except his own personal indulgence. Drugs rapidly became a habit and, added to the drinking, reduced him to a condition bordering on insanity. He resorted to every petty trick, every ignoble excuse, to obtain opium. He wheedled the money for the purpose from his father who, rather than face the violence of Branwell's moods, gave the money while praying for Branwell's soul. He became involved in debts that brought the bailiff to the house, and fearing the indignity of their brother's arrest the sisters paid the amount owing, keeping the disgrace from Mr. Brontë.

But such self-destruction was bound to have an end. In the summer of 1848, Branwell had his first attacks of delirium tremens, described by Mrs. Gaskell as "most frightful in character." The young man's constitution was completely broken, and the last phase was inevitable. Mr. Brontë continually urged the consolation and redemption of prayer, but his son would hear none of it. With wild bravado he insisted he would die on his feet, cursing his fate. However, to Mr.

116

Haworth Parsonage from the Church. *Copyright, Walter Scott.*

Haworth Parsonage. *Copyright, Walter Scott.*

View of the Moors. *Copyright, Walter Scott.*

View taken from a pond opposite the Brontë Falls. *Copyright, Walter Scott.*

Brontë's great comfort, they prayed together at the end. Branwell died on the twenty-fourth of September, 1848. Charlotte's letter to Mr. Williams, written a week after his death, is fitting epitaph to her brother's brief and blighted life. When all is said and done, there was no one like Charlotte for looking things straight in the eye, and summing them up with a radiant perception of the truth, regardless of the emotional implications.

> We have hurried our dead out of our sight. A lull begins to succeed the gloomy tumult of last week. It is not permitted us to grieve for him who is gone as others grieve for those they lose. The removal of our only brother must necessarily be regarded by us rather in the light of mercy than a chastisement. Branwell was his father's and his sisters' pride and hope in boyhood, but since manhood the case has been otherwise. It has been our lot to see him take a wrong bent; to hope, expect, wait his return to the right path; to know the sickness of hope deferred, the dismay of prayer baffled; to experience despair at last— and now to behold the sudden early obscure close of what might have been a noble career.

> I do not weep from a sense of bereavement—there is no prop withdrawn, no consolation torn away, no dear companion lost—but for the wreck of talent, the ruin of promise, the untimely dreary extinction of what might have been a burning and a shining light. My brother was a year my junior. I had aspirations and ambitions for him once, long ago—they have perished mournfully. Nothing remains of him but a memory of errors and sufferings. There is such a bitterness of pity for his life and death, such a yearning for the emptiness of his whole existence as I cannot describe. I trust time will allay these feelings.

> My poor father naturally thought more of his *only* son

than of his daughters, and, much and long as he had suffered on his account, he cried out for his loss like David for that of Absalom—my son! my son!—and refused at first to be comforted. And then when I ought to have been able to collect my strength and be at hand to support him, I fell ill with an illness whose approaches I had felt for some time previously, and of which the crisis was hastened by the awe and trouble of the death-scene—the first I had ever witnessed. The past has seemed to me a strange week. Thank God, for my father's sake, I am better now, though still feeble. I wish indeed I had more general strength—the want of it is sadly in my way. I cannot do what I would do for want of sustained animal spirits and efficient vigour.

My unhappy brother never knew what his sisters had done in literature—he was not aware that they had ever published a line. We could not tell him of our efforts for fear of causing him too deep a pang of remorse for his own time, and talents misapplied. Now he will *never* know. I cannot dwell longer on the subject at present—it is too painful.

*Chapter* XIII  FIRST PUBLICATION:
POEMS BY CURRER, ELLIS,
AND ACTON BELL

IN THE preface to a new edition of *Wuthering Heights and Agnes Grey*, published in 1850, Charlotte writes:

> One day, in the autumn of 1845, I accidentally lighted on a MS. of verse in my sister Emily's handwriting. Of course, I was not surprised, knowing that she did and could write verse. I looked it over, and something more than surprise seized me—a deep conviction that these were not common effusions, nor at all like the poetry women write. I thought them condensed and terse, vigorous and genuine. To my ear they had also a peculiar music, wild, melancholy, and elevating. My sister Emily was not a person of demonstrative character, nor one on the recesses of whose mind and feelings even those nearest and dearest to her could, with impunity, intrude unlicensed. It took hours to reconcile her to the discovery I had made, and days to persuade her that such poems merited publication."

Perhaps Charlotte did come across the poems accidentally. Or perhaps she suspected their existence and went looking for them. Emily's apparent anger might indicate the latter. However, it would have been like Emily to be displeased at this invasion of her privacy, even supposing Charlotte had

**119**

found the poems by chance. And Charlotte, knowing her sister's feelings about personal matters, particularly writing, should have returned the poems to their hiding place and said nothing to Emily about them. Instead, Charlotte seems to have been struck with an idea as soon as she realized the unusual quality of the poems themselves. Why not publish them! All three sisters had "early cherished the dream," as Charlotte says, "of one day being authors." Perhaps one (or two or three) of them would become famous. How wonderful that would be. And now here was some writing that Charlotte, at least, felt convinced, after a single reading, was worthy of meeting the public eye.

As Charlotte said, it was not so easy to convince Emily. How she succeeded in breaking down Emily's objections, what arguments she used, she doesn't say. But she had no more than persuaded Emily that she must try publication than Anne "quietly produced," some poems of her own, and, Charlotte confessed, *she* had been writing poetry, too. What a coincidence! All three sisters, it seems, had been indulging in verse writing, more or less in secret. Now it was out in the open, and enough for a book done in collaboration. Publication seemed the only logical answer.

It was Charlotte who took the initiative in making the necessary arrangements, preparing the material in proper form, and sending it to a publisher. They all agreed that "authoresses are liable to be looked upon with prejudice," and so decided to conceal themselves by "assuming Christian names positively masculine." Such a subterfuge would also relieve them of the embarrassment of publicity, which was something that young ladies of the day felt it a duty to eschew. The names chosen were Currer, Ellis, and Acton Bell,

120

pseudonyms for Charlotte, Emily, and Anne Brontë respectively.

The next step was to find a publisher who would bring the book out, if not at his own risk, at least at the authors'. Charlotte wrote Messrs. Chambers of Edinburgh. Failing to receive any answer whatsoever, she next approached Messrs. Aylott and Jones of Paternoster Row, London. Aylott and Jones eventually agreed to bring out the book at a cost of 31 pounds 10 shillings. One might wonder where the sisters obtained such a sum of money, which, though not large, was still a great deal for a family of small means to invest. It came from the modest legacy left them by Aunt Elizabeth, the same Aunt Elizabeth who had, before her death, loaned them the money which enabled Charlotte and Emily to attend school in Brussels. They had used the legacy to buy railroad shares, and these provided enough to pay the costs of publication.

During the proofreading and printing, which took considerable time, a rather voluminous correspondence developed between Charlotte and the publishers, and these letters can be found in Mr. Clement Shorter's *Charlotte Brontë and Her Circle*. Charlotte had taken pains to inform herself on typography and format, and had no hesitation in making suggestions. She estimated that the book would run to 200 or 250 pages, and she wished it to be an octavo volume resembling Moxon's latest edition of Wordsworth. When told that the manuscript would not require such a large volume, Charlotte writes, "The MS. will certainly form a thinner volume than I had anticipated. I cannot name another model which I would like it precisely to resemble; yet, I think, a duodecimo form, and a somewhat reduced, though still *clear* type, would be preferable. I only stipulate for *clear* type.

not too small, and good paper." She always signed herself C. Brontë, and, since there was no meeting between author and publisher, the Messrs. Aylott and Jones must have been somewhat mystified as to the identity of Currer, Ellis, and Acton Bell. Charlotte's only explanation had been, "You will perceive that the poems are the work of three persons, relatives—their separate pieces are distinguished by their respective signatures." One imagines that the publishers may have decided that the signatory was a wealthy patron of letters who thought he had discovered genius.

Toward the end of May, 1846, *Poems by Currer, Ellis and Acton Bell* was published, having "stolen into life" as Mrs. Gaskell describes it. It may be said to have stolen out also. For almost a year later Charlotte, still keeping in character as Currer Bell, confessed in a letter to Thomas de Quincy that only two copies of the book had been sold outright. With the letter went a presentation copy, possibly in the hope that Mr. de Quincy might be moved to speak favorably of the book in the press, or by return post. She wrote:

Sir—, My relatives, Ellis and Acton Bell, and myself, heedless of the repeated warnings of various respectful publishers, have committed the rash act of printing a volume of poems.

The consequences predicted have, of course, overtaken us. Our book is bound to be a drug; no man needs it or heeds it. In the space of a year our publisher has disposed but of two copies, and by what painful efforts he succeeded in getting rid of these two, himself only knows.

Before transferring the edition to the trunkmakers, we have decided on distributing as presents a few copies of what we cannot sell; and we beg to offer you one in acknowledgement of the pleasure and profit we have often and long derived from your works. I am, yours very respectfully, Currer Bell.

But, although there was the heartbreaking fact that only two people in England had been brave enough to buy a book of poetry by three unknown writers, there were certain compensations for this rash act of publishing. Reviews appearing in the *Critic* and *Athenaeum* were sufficiently favorable to tempt the Messrs. Bell into spending an additional ten pounds for advertising. The advertisements were to include a quotation from the *Critic*: "They in whose hearts are chords strung by nature to sympathise with the beautiful and true, will recognize in these compositions the presence of more genius than it was supposed this utilitarian age had devoted to the loftier exercises of the intellect." And three months later Charlotte wrote an appreciative letter to the editor of the *Dublin University Magazine* thanking him for the generous review the magazine had given the book.

Sir,— I thank you in my own name and that of my brothers, Ellis and Acton, for the indulgent notice that appeared in your last number of our first humble efforts in literature; but I thank you far more for the essay on modern poetry which preceded that notice—an essay in which seems to me to be condensed the very spirit of truth and beauty. If all or half of your other readers shall have derived from its perusal the delight it afforded myself and my brothers, your labors have produced a rich result.

After such criticism an author may indeed be smitten at first by a sense of his own insignificance, as it were, but on a second and third perusal he finds a power and beauty therein which stirs him to a desire to do more and better things. It fulfills the right end of criticism. Without absolutely crushing, it corrects and rouses. I again thank you heartily, and beg to subscribe myself,— Your constant and grateful reader, Currer Bell.

There is a sincere humility in such a letter, and no bitterness at all. There is not even an appeal for pity, or any note of self-pity. Actually, the sisters felt none. The publication of their book had fulfilled the dream they had cherished of one day being authors. To them the fact that a book of theirs was in print made them authors. They did not go beyond that, even to doubt the publishers' enterprise in having done no better in sales promotion. They doubted the value of the writing instead. In the same preface to the 1850 edition of *Wuthering Heights and Agnes Grey* referred to above, Charlotte says, "The book was printed; and all of it that merits to be known are the poems of Ellis Bell. The fixed conviction I held, and hold, of the worth of these poems has not, indeed, received the confirmation of much favorable criticism; but I must retain it not withstanding."

Charlotte was right, as usual. Posterity would one day prove how right she was. But both sisters were sensible enough to take a first failure with calm good nature, without prejudice, and with malice toward none. They had scarcely thought of consigning the unsold copies of *Poems by Currer, Ellis and Acton Bell* to the trunkmaker than they were hard at work on their first novels, Charlotte on *The Professor,* Emily on *Wuthering Heights,* and Anne on *Agnes Grey.*

*Chapter* xiv   THE PROFESSOR

*The Professor* was the first of the four novels writen by Charlotte Brontë, though it was not published until two years after her death. It is regarded as the least representative of her genius. And yet its qualities are, one feels, entirely within the scale of her intention. She tells the story, not so much with an eye to values, as with an earnest concern for characteristics. The setting and the circumstances, these are what compelled her. How were the characters moved by environment and incident, she asked herself. The effect is a tapestry done in dull shades, but the lines, though thin, are clear and unwavering. She made no attempt to get under the skin of her characters. *The Professor* is a story of exteriors. Here and there she came close to dipping below surfaces to passionate abandon. But something held her in check, a certain fear of letting go. Therefore the novel is more intellectual than it is psychological or emotional. Which is, of course, what has caused Rebecca West to say, "Color is lent to the suspicion that Charlotte Brontë is not an artist but a sub-artist, that she does not analyze experience, but weaves fantasies to hang between man and his painful experience by the frequent use of the sub-artist's chosen weapon, sentimental writing. Charlotte Brontë was a supreme artist; and yet she was very nearly not an artist at all." And one wonders why it is that sentimentality, as it

125

seeps through the pages of *The Professor,* and flattens, as must be admitted, many pages of *Jane Eyre* and *Shirley,* has so damaged Charlotte Brontë's reputation, when, with many another great author, it is a forgiven indulgence.

There is a great difference of opinion with regard to *The Professor.* Is it a work of art, worthy of the woman who was to write *Jane Eyre* and *Villette?* I think so. I think it gives more than a hint of the later power, and I think the manner of writing was well intended. Charlotte was not "giving a loose to her soul" until she had perfected the mold into which to pour it. She was still a prey to her habitual caution; she dared not let out the rein. May Sinclair claims that it was only after Charlotte had seen the manuscript of Emily's *Wuthering Heights* that she threw caution to the winds and gave her imagination full sway. The result was *Jane Eyre.*

My opinion is that *The Professor* deserves more praise, a wider audience, than it has received, in spite of the sentimentality which we grant is there in too large a measure. The characters of Frances Henri and William Crimsworth are drawn with very deft and subtle touches and, though she has not penetrated to any passionate depths, she has redeemed them from bathos. They are not types, but personalities. And *The Professor* contains superb passages of description, as fine as Charlotte ever wrote.

Charlotte herself did not think ill of her first novel. Neither did she ask "indulgence for it on the plea of a first attempt, for that," she declared, "it certainly was not, as the pen that wrote it had been previously worn in practice of some years." She was naturally referring to the practice in writing she had had during the voluminous chapters of the *Young Men's Play* and the Angrian romances. Such early and vigorous discipline at least justifies her in affirming: "I had got over any such taste as I might have had for ornamented and decorated composition, and come to prefer what was plain and homely." This was the choice that explains the characters of *The Professor,* a choice that made her argue with Emily and Anne that a heroine need not be beautiful to be both worthy and interesting, and that the aspiration and fortitude of the spirit are more important than fascination and charm of feature. Yes, Charlotte knew what she was doing in her art as she knew what she was doing in life! If *The Professor* has a major fault it is that her calculation shows through the material, as it doesn't in her later work.

*The Professor* grew out of Charlotte Brontë's experiences in Brussels, as did *Villette,* the greater of the two books, which dealt with a heroine tossed on the seas of passion and suffering. But Frances Henri was the forerunner of Lucy Stowe, as William Crimsworth was, to a certain degree, of M. Paul Emanuel. *The Professor* is a novel of two parts, the scene of the first being laid in England, and that of the second in Brussels. The plot is also somewhat divided. In England the story revolves about the lives of two brothers, unlike each other in every way. Edward, the elder, operates a mill in which William, the younger, works. But the occupation and environment are completely at variance with William's tastes and interests, so that a strong antagonism develops between the brothers. Eventually there is a final break, and William departs for Brussels, where he becomes a teacher in M. Pelet's school for boys. And in Brussels he meets Frances Henri, and falls in love. The remainder of the book is the story of their romance against the foreign background that had so deeply affected Charlotte.

We are not led to expect passion from the contained spirit, the calm intelligence, of Frances Henri. And she does not

127

waken it in William Crimsworth. Yet there is a kind of idyllic appeal in the love affair of these two, which springs from what Charlotte describes as the "delicious solidarity" of the young lady, and the decorous reserve of her lover. And the scene in which William, having come into a small competence, indicates his wish to marry Frances, is expressive of Charlotte's own philosophy of matrimony:

> "Think of marrying you to be kept by you, Monsieur! I could not do it; and how dull my days would be! You would be away teaching in close, noisy schoolrooms, from morning till evening, and I should be lingering at home, unemployed and solitary. I should get depressed and sullen, and you would tire of me."
>
> "Frances, you could yet read and study—two things you like so well."
>
> "Monsieur, I could not, I like a contemplative life, but I like an active better; I must act in some way, and act with you. I have taken notice, Monsieur, that people who act only in each others' company for amusement, never really like each other so well, or esteem each other so highly, as those who work together, and perhaps suffer together!"
>
> "You speak God's truth [Crimsworth replies], and you shall have your own way, for it is the best way."

*The Professor* has no plot in the conventional sense. It might more properly be said to be a series of vignettes. The dialogue makes them that: an arrangement of tableaus or scenes. They are meant to illustrate the relationship between the lovers rather than to interpret their feelings. One receives a certain delight from the deft flourishes of the pen, whether in conversation or in description, but the strokes are at their best in the descriptive passages. These last give us Charlotte's poetic spirit in its true colors. Her own poetry was mediocre, for she was unable, as Emily, to fit matter to form with her sister's genius; but given the unhampered freedom of prose, her poetic imagination took flight. Her word painting is exquisite. Such descriptive passages as the one we quote lift the story into literature, in spite of the qualities it lacks as a novel:

Already the pavement was drying; a balmy and fresh breeze stirred the air, purified by lightning; I left the west behind me, where a spread sky like opal, azure inmingled with crimson; the enlarged sun, glorious in Tyrian dyes, dipped his brim already; stepping, as I was, eastward, I faced a vast bank of clouds, but also I had before me the arch of an even rainbow; a perfect rainbow—high, wide, vivid. I looked long; my eye drank in the scene, and I suppose my brain must have absorbed it; for that night, after lying awake in pleasant fever a long time, watching the silent sheet-lightning, which still played among the retreating clouds, and flashed silvery over the stars, I at last fell asleep; and then in a dream was reproduced the setting sun, the bank of clouds, the mighty rainbow. I stood, methought, on a terrace; I leaned over a parapeted wall; there was space below me, depth I could not fathom, but hearing an endless splash of waves, I believed it to be the sea; sea spread to the horizon; sea of changeful green and intense blue; all was soft in the distance; all vapour-veiled. A spark of gold glistened on the line between water and air, floated up, appeared, enlarged and changed; the object hung midway between heaven and earth, under the arch of the rainbow; the soft but dark clouds diffused behind. It hovered as on wings; pearly, fleecy, gleaming air streamed like raiment round it; light, tinted with carnation, coloured what seemed face and limbs; a large star shone with still lustre on an angel's forehead.

Yet no publisher would take *The Professor*. It went the heartbreaking rounds from office to office. This journey of the manuscript best illustrates a certain naïveté in Charlotte that she never outgrew, with all her shrewd arrangement of life. She never took the trouble to change the wrapping on the bundle of sheets in which they were returned from the latest publisher! She would merely erase as best she could, and send it forth again. Such a purity of intention, whereby there is no attempt to conceal one's failures in order to further one's success, is a tribute to the character and integrity of a great nature. Emily and Anne possessed the same virtue to an even higher degree. It is a quality the world could well emulate in these days of propaganda.

When the manuscript reached Smith, Elder, Mr. Williams of the firm's editorial staff also rejected it, not for lack of merit, he said, but because it was too short for the average three-volume novel. It was a period when the longer the better, the reader demanding his money's worth in number of pages and volumes. This rejection, however, established a correspondence between Charlotte and Mr. Williams that led to his becoming her friend and literary mentor, and to the publication of *Jane Eyre* by the firm of Smith, Elder.

"To come to *Jane Eyre* after *The Professor*, declares May Sinclair, "is to pass into another world of feeling and vision." But the two worlds are linked by the symbol of the rue d'Isabelle, that was like a river of dreams flowing through Charlotte's heart bearing strange crafts of human experience.

*Chapter* xv  JANE EYRE

I N March, 1847, shortly before her thirty-first birthday, Charlotte Brontë wrote her friend Ellen Nussey, "I shall be thirty-one next birthday. My youth is gone like a dream; and very little use have I even made of it. What have I done these last thirty years? Precious little." Yet, only a few months later, she was to realize in full what those years had meant. For in the first week of October, 1847, an unknown novelist by the name of Currer Bell gave the world a story called *Jane Eyre.*

When, as we previously noted, Mr. Williams of Smith, Elder turned down *The Professor,* he was cordially regretful, and expressed the hope that Currer Bell would grant him the pleasure of examining any future work, particularly if it was of greater length. Charlotte, nothing daunted by what might have appeared merely a kind way of giving her the brush-off, as we say today, took him at his word, and wrote immediately to say she had a three-volume novel in the making which she hoped to finish within a month. When the completed *Jane Eyre* reached Mr. Williams, he is said to have given it his entire attention, to the exclusion of all else, until he finished it. "He was so powerfully struck by the character of the tale," Mrs. Gaskell writes, "that he reported his impression in very strong terms to Mr. Smith, who appears to have been much amused by the admiration excited. 'You

131

seem to have been so enchanted, that I do not know how to believe you,' he laughingly said. But when a second reader (the Mr. Taylor who later proposed to Charlotte), a clear-headed Scotchman not given to enthusiasm, had taken the MS. home in the evening, and become so deeply interested in it as to sit up half the night to finish it, Mr. Smith's curiosity was sufficiently excited to prompt him to read it for himself; and great as were the praises which had been bestowed upon it, he found that they had not exceeded the truth." So Mr. Smith of Smith, Elder promptly published it, and thereby was responsible for turning a page in the history of the novel, and, more than that, in the history of womankind.

Nothing like this novel had ever come from the hand of a woman, in English, or any other, literature. Her predecessors, Fanny Burney, Ann Radcliffe, Maria Edgeworth, Jane Porter, and Jane Austen, her contemporaries Mrs. Oliphant, Mrs. Gaskell, and George Eliot, had enriched English fiction to be sure, but not with the electrifying dramatic effect produced by *Jane Eyre*. Charlotte Brontë shot her bolt at the very heart of Victorian complacency and opened up a seething subconscious of feminine revolt against convention, of suppressed humiliations and resentments, that women had been nourishing in their breasts far too long. And it was not merely the individual that it probed, exposing, like a surgeon's knife, the quivering nerves of the passionate anatomy of woman's nature, but the institutions that had imprisoned her for their own security and survival.

One of the extraordinary things about the reception of *Jane Eyre* was that it fascinated, at the same time that it repelled, the mind and sense of its generation. As popular entertainment its reception was tremendous, overriding all critical censure and disapproval. It swept the emotions of its readers before it in a flood of sensations that had previously been kept in the dark, in more ways than one, if felt at all. Its realism challenged the professional critics. The public had not had its feelings so ruthlessly stirred since Byron gave them romantic passion in his narrative verse. Previously, when anyone wished to lay bare the soul of man, he resorted to the safer smokescreen of poetry. But lately the novel had begun to realize its power to investigate the inner conflicts, the capacities for joy and grief, love and hate, that human flesh is heir to. Charlotte Brontë, largely because she was blissfully unaware of the depths below her, went overboard. The result was furiously controversial, in and out of the press.

Of course the critics, being male, or women who, like Miss Rigby, prided themselves on going one step further in repudiating their own sex, felt it their bounden duty to be shocked at the moral and social aspects involved. That Jane Eyre, not only a woman, but a woman of low degree, should attempt to probe the human frailties of men *and* women, the qualities of character that are effected by the relationship between the sexes, and particularly the passion that is as much a right of women as men—this was too much for the male ego to accept without protest. God forbid that women should be encouraged to follow in Jane's footsteps, or that such a fantastic emotional outburst should be mistaken for real life. The possibility must be nipped in the bud. Not that the pleasure of nipping it in the bud wasn't given fresh impetus by the necessity for reading the book. Naturally one has to read what one censors—even in Boston!

One of the earliest and most venomous attacks appeared in *The Quarterly Review*. John T. Lockhart, editor of the *Quarterly*, had sent a review copy of *Jane Eyre* to Miss Rigby (who later became Lady Eastlake), together with Thackeray's *Vanity Fair* and a treatise on schools entitled *Governesses*. The letter he wrote, enclosing them, is most interesting in view of what had happened previously, and of the events that were to occur:

> About three years ago I received a small volume of *Poems by Currer, Ellis and Acton Bell,* and a queer little note by Currer Bell who said the book had been published a year, and just two copies sold, so they were to burn the rest, but distributed a few copies, mine being one. I find what seems rather a fair review of that tiny tome in the *Spectator* of this week; pray look at it.
>
> I think the poems of Currer much better than those of Acton and Ellis, and believe his novel is vastly better than those which they have more recently put forth.
>
> I know nothing of the writers, but the common rumor is that they are brothers of the weaving order in some Lancashire town. At first it was generally said Currer was a lady, and Mayfair circumstantialised by making her the *chere amie* of Mr. Thackeray. But your skill in "dress" settles the question of sex. I think, however, some woman must have assisted in the school scenes of *Jane Eyre,* which have a striking air of truthfulness to me—an ignoramus, I allow, on such points.
>
> I should say you might well glance at the novels by Acton and Ellis Bell—*Wuthering Heights* is one of them. If you have any friend about Manchester, it would, I suppose, be easy to learn accurately as to the position of these men.

Whether Miss Rigby actually wrote the review which resulted from this assignment is somewhat questionable. There is a possibility, vouched for by Mr. Andrew Lang, that a certain Mr. Brocklebank, "a black-marble clergyman," either wrote the article or collaborated with Miss Rigby. And it would seem highly probable that Mr. Lang was right. The hand of the clergy appears to be discernible in the harsh tones of the denunciation. After all, the attitude would have the approval of such an eminent authority of the cloth as Charles Kingsley, whose word for Jane Eyre was "coarse."

We have said [writes Miss Rigby (or Mr. Brockle-bank)] that this was a picture of a natural heart. This, to our view, is the great and crying mischief of the book. *Jane Eyre* is throughout the personification of an unre-generate and undisciplined spirit—the more dangerous to exhibit from that prestige of principle and self-control which is liable to dazzle the eye too much for it to observe the insufficient and unsound foundation on which it rests. It is true that Jane does right, and exerts great moral strength, but it is the strength of a mere heathen mind, which is a law unto itself. No Christian grace is percep-tible upon her. She has inherited in the fullest measure the worst sin of our fallen nature, the sin of pride. Jane Eyre is proud, and therefore she is ungrateful too. It pleased God to make her an orphan, friendless and penni-less, and yet she thanks nobody, least of all the friends, companions, and instructors of her helpless youth, for the food and raiment, the care and education, vouchsafed to her till she was capable in mind and fit to provide for herself. Altogether the autobiography of Jane Eyre is pre-eminently an anti-Christian composition. There is throughout it a murmuring against the comforts of the rich and the privations of the poor, which, so far as each individual is concerned, is a murmuring against God's appointment. There is a proud and perpetual asserting of the rights of man for which we find no authority in God's Word or His Providence. There is that pervading tone of ungodly discontent which is at once the most prominent and the most subtle evil which the law and the pulpit, which all civilized society, in fact, at the present day has to contend with.

The *Quarterly* also was of two minds as to the sex of the author of *Jane Eyre*. Was Currer Bell man or woman? "No woman," the reviewer states emphatically, "trusses game, garnishes dessert dishes with the same hands, or talks of doing so in the same breath. Above all, no woman attires another in such fancy dresses as Jane's ladies assume. Miss Ingram coming down irresistible in a *morning* robe of sky-blue crepe, a gauze azure scarf twisted in her hair! No lady, we understand, when suddenly aroused in the night, would think of hurrying on 'a frock.' They have garments more convenient for such occasions, and more becoming, too!" Obviously believing that the author is not only a man, but a dangerous and fanatic radical as well, the reviewer continues: "We do not hesitate to say that the tone of mind and thought which has overthrown authority, and violated every code, human and divine, abroad, and fostered chartism and rebellion at home, is the same which has also written *Jane Eyre*." And "he" goes on to make what Miss May Sinclair calls "an infamous and immoral utterance": "If we ascribe the book to a woman at all, we have no alternative but to ascribe it to one who has, for some sufficient reason, long forfeited the society of her own sex."

What was this story that stirred such passions in the hearts of its readers? Where did it spring from, whether from the heart of man or woman, out of what travail and faith? Actually the fictional character of Jane Eyre is a tangled web of autobiographical counterpoint. Jane Eyre's recital of her life, and of her love for the master of Thornfield, was drawn directly from the realities of Charlotte Brontë's life. The atmosphere was one she had known and absorbed; the situations were those she had observed intimately, suffered, and not accepted; the characters had many of them been ripening through the long apprenticeship of the Angrian cycle. Charlotte's sources and resources were so rich and varied it is not surprising she sometimes became embarrassed in the use of them when attempting the novel form. She had always freely piled incident on incident, character on character, in haphazard abandonment to imaginative impulses. Now incident and character must be harnessed tandem to a vehicle she had never ridden. So that while her creative genius easily transformed the illusions of Angria to the realities of Thornfield, it still could fail to keep the course of action in proper focus and perspective. From the exteriors and intellectual refinements of *The Professor,* she leaped with a sudden and direct force into the interiors and passions of *Jane Eyre;* and, dazed by the transition, she had difficulty to keep her narrative in balance, her values defined. Her fortitude, however, sustained her, and she persisted until the essence of passion, and it was a profoundly *spiritual passion,* yielded its strong magic to flavor the crises in the love of Jane and Rochester. As May Sinclair says in her introduction to the 1905 edition of *Jane Eyre,* published by J. M. Dent, London:

> Passion was Charlotte Brontë's secret. She gave a new meaning to the word. She was the first novelist to handle the thing, the real thing. Jane Austen was not alone in her ignorance of it. None of the older novelists had treated it adequately. For Scott it was simply a high, vague, romantic feeling that hung round his characters like a dress. Richardson got somewhere near it in *Clarissa*

*Harlowe* without knowing it. His vision was impaired by the damp fog of sentiment in which he loved to live. To Fielding passion meant animal passion, and as such he rightly held it unimportant.

For Thackeray, too, it is a sharp fever of the senses, to be treated with the brevity its episodic and accidental character deserves.

None of these novelists understood by passion what Charlotte Brontë understood. And the comfortable, sentimental, thoroughly prosaic Early Victorians who devoured *Jane Eyre* did not understand it either and were shocked.

Beginning as the orphan child with the Reeds at Gateshead, where her spirit was wounded by the frightful experience of the Red Room, to the finding of the blind and broken Rochester, and the atonement of her marriage to him, Jane Eyre tells her story in a series of poignant crises. As a child of ten, she confesses, "I was a discord at Gateshead." This is the motif of an autobiography. Jane was out of step with life, she was a discord in the harmony of love and convention, off-key in her adjustment to society, so-called. Yet all these discordant notes were to be resolved in what Miss Sinclair calls a "truth beyond reality."

I think one is first made aware of the symbolic significance of certain episodes, that weave an oft-repeated melody throughout the whole, at the first meeting of Jane and Rochester. Eight years after Jane leaves the infamous school at Lowood, and goes out into the world to make a living, we find her at Thornfield as governess to Adele Varens, the half-French half-English ward of Rochester. Rochester has been absent from Thornfield at the time Mrs. Fairfax, the household manager, engaged her. When he returns, he meets with an accident on the icy path approaching the house, spraining an ankle. Jane goes to his assistance, and though he is a strong, heavy man, leaning on her frail body he is safely helped indoors. Here, from the first, we have the interplay, the juxtaposition, of the forces that make the novel so powerful and stimulating: the superior power of the spirit, particularly when it is aflame with love, over the instability of matter. Charlotte clearly conceived this idea as being the guiding thread that held together and unified the novel, not as incidents in a consciously "invented" plot, but as abstractions released from the secret frustrations of the heart.

There are four such crises in *Jane Eyre,* rising like snow-capped peaks lit by the rays of a setting sun. By way of these, the soul of Jane, as in *Pilgrim's Progress,* reaches successive heights of self-sacrifice and redemption, gains a discipline over the turbulent spirit, attains ultimate happiness and rest. The first of these, already referred to, was the terror she experienced as a child in the Red Room at Gateshead; the second was the severe trial her love for Rochester suffered at his hands at Thornfield; the third, the telepathic exchange between them that impelled their meeting, the spirit of each yearning for revelation; and, finally, Jane's triumph over temptation when it became clear she could not marry Rochester. Charlotte Brontë, in her handling of these episodes, seems to be exercising her most rigid Calvinistic convictions to catechize the waywardness of the human heart. Yet when she discovers that man's seeming desire to break the laws of nature is really only his need to break the laws of man, she grants her characters mercy and salvation. The "values" of Gateshead were conventions, she discovers, not the laws that should underlie the obligations of both domestic and Christian life. Although the intolerable conditions at Lowood were a sin against Christian principles, the worst that could be said of them was that they were mistaken, yet they had foundation in the creed in which Charlotte believed: it is God's will to chasten with trial and pain those whom He most loves.

As I have said, there is so much in *Jane Eyre* that is subject to symbolic interpretation. And it is all encompassed by the great house at Thornfield, whose destruction by fire is itself an emblem. The whole drama of Jane's love is played out in this house. Through its rooms wander the brutal spirit of Rochester's cruel deception; the delicate charm and innocence of Adele, the illegitimate child; the tipsy ogre; Grace Poole; Bertha, the mad wife, confined to her chamber of horrors; and the gentle, graceful Mrs. Fairfax. The child Adele is perhaps the most symbolic of all Charlotte Brontë's characters. Adele is the symbol of that purity which sin may beget but cannot harm, when the sin is an accident of man's nature caught in the grip of natural law—that force which is an expression of God's will to create. As the symbol of the expiation of such "sin," Charlotte's Adele is the first in fiction, to be followed closely by Pearl in *The Scarlet Letter*. But Charlotte's portrait is perhaps even more vivid, and certainly as beautiful, as Hawthorne's.

Furthermore there are whole conversations that are, in themselves, an interpretation, a symbolic representation, of an idea. Take, for instance, the conversation that follows Jane's discovery of Rochester's philandering with Blanche Ingram:

> "I grieve to leave Thornfield [says Jane], I love Thornfield:—I love it because I have lived in it a full and delightful life,—momentarily, at least. I have not been trampled on. I have not been petrified. I have not been

buried with inferior minds, and excluded from every glimpse of communion with what is bright and energetic and high. I have talked, face to face, with what I reverence; with what I delight in—with an original, a vigorous, an expanded mind. I have known you, Mr. Rochester; and it strikes me with terror and anguish to feel I absolutely must be torn from you for ever. I see the necessity of departure; and it is like looking on the necessity of death."

"Where do you see the necessity?" he asked, suddenly.

"Where? You, sir, have placed it before me."

"In what shape?"

"In the shape of Miss Ingram; a noble and beautiful woman,—your bride."

"My bride! What bride? I have no bride!"

"But you will have."

"Yes;—I will!" He set his teeth.

"Then I must go:—you have said it yourself."

"No; you must stay! I swear it—and the oath shall be kept."

"I tell you I must go!" I retorted, roused to something like passion. "Do you think I can stay to become nothing to you? Do you think I am an automaton?—a machine without feelings? and can bear to have my morsel of bread snatched from my lips, and my drop of living water dashed from my cup? Do you think, because I am poor, obscure, plain, little, I am soulless and heartless? You think wrong!—I have as much soul as you,—and full as much heart! And if God had gifted me with some beauty, and much wealth, I should have made it as hard for you to leave me, as it is now for me to leave you. I am not talking to you now through the medium of custom, conventionalities, or even of mortal flesh:—it is my spirit that addresses your spirit; just as if both had passed through

141

the grave and we stood at God's feet equal,—as we are!"
"As we are!" repeated Mr. Rochester.

The critics have been immensely disturbed by this passage, objecting to its psychology and its histrionics. Charlotte herself was interested in neither. She knew nothing of the former, and cared nothing for the latter. Her concern was entirely with the moralities of love and passion, those emotions that compel man to reach the most exalted place life can hold or to sink to its most despicable depths; and her principle of morality was not found in any system devised by man, as Miss Sinclair said, but came from a divine source which embraces the whole of creation. In this dialogue she gave vent to that pride which was considered the unpardonable sin of the orphaned and the helpless. It was Charlotte's mission to tumble the mighty from their seats, and exalt the lowly and meek. The meek shall have pride, she says, if it is purified with the emotions that are the common heritage of all men—and women. She also was moved by an immense sympathy for the suffering of the human soul, heart, and mind. Whereas Becky Sharpe, of *Vanity Fair,* has lost much of her original glamour, having been made an object of dislike and satire by her creator, Jane Eyre has emerged steadily brighter, due to the pity and understanding that Charlotte's conscience, incapable of ethical infidelity, poured upon her. To quote again from Miss Sinclair:

What, after all, was the passion that Charlotte understood? It is not any blind, unspiritual instinct. Her Jane's upward gaze is "the very sublime of faith, truth and devotion." She has not only shown in Jane the power of passion. She was the first to vindicate its essential purity; the first woman to divine that a woman's passion, when complete, is two-fold, she being destined supremely for maternity. In Charlotte Brontë's hands passion becomes a thing of strange innocences and tendernesses and terrors, rejoicing in service and the sacrifice of self. A thing superbly unaware of animal instinct; a profound and tragic thing that bears at its heart the prescience of suffering and of death.

Because of this quality in her, little Jane, in spite of her quaint and somewhat alienating precision, and her tendency to refer to herself as a "dependent," remains to this day young and splendid and modern to her fingertips.

*Chapter* XVI **SHIRLEY**

CHARLOTTE BRONTË's novels are all studies of women against the Victorian background of England, a background not so much of a period as of a convention. But whereas Jane Eyre and Lucy Snowe are presented subjectively, autobiographically, Shirley Keeldar is an objective portrayal. Charlotte holds Shirley off, as it were, for scrutiny, and for that reason Shirley is spared the brush strokes of sentimentality that sometimes dull the canvas of *Jane Eyre*. Also the atmosphere of place, the Yorkshire scene, exerts a more vital influence on the whole picture of *Shirley*. Indeed, scene is greatly responsible for Shirley's attractive personality, for the fascination she has for everyone who comes to know her. And I agree with the critics who say that the underlying reason for Shirley's character being what it is, her steadfast soul and its oneness with steadfast nature, is that Emily was the model Charlotte used. I do not agree that the character of Shirley is a failure because it is only a partly realized delineation of Emily, as some have said, for it seems to me that what there is of Emily in Shirley is a phantom spirit that emerges in those rare moments when the girl is transported by the supreme beauty in nature. Charlotte herself says that she thought of Emily as she wrote of Shirley. But the question remains, did she have Emily in mind from the beginning, or did Emily find her way into the book as

144

she progressed? The latter seems more likely, since the writing was begun before Emily's death. It would seem that, later in the book, memories of her sister were what gave the character of Shirley its poignant qualities, its spiritual significance. As Miss Ratchford says, Shirley Keeldar is what Emily "might have been had she known health and prosperity."

It was during the writing of *Shirley* that Charlotte passed through "The Valley of the Shadow of Death," to use the title of her twenty-fourth chapter, taken in turn from *Pilgrim's Progress*. She had the novel about half completed when Emily became mortally ill, and her death was followed swiftly by Anne's. Charlotte had laid the manuscript aside during this tragic period of illness and death. She had taken Anne to Scarborough in the hope that the sea air would be a healing influence. But the tuberculosis, that scourge of the Brontë family, again took its toll, and Charlotte returned to the empty parsonage at Haworth bowed with grief and loneliness. "I felt that the house was all silent," she wrote Ellen Nussey, "the rooms were all empty. I remembered where the three were laid—in what dark narrow dwellings—nevermore to reappear on earth.... The agony that was to be undergone, and was not to be avoided, came on. I underwent it, and passed a dreary evening and night, and a mournful morrow." It is difficult to conceive such tragedy visited upon one so young, so solitary, and so isolated.

What this "agony to be undergone" did to Charlotte was to force her to reconceive her novel, and make of the second part a memorial to her sister Emily. There is no doubt that she set herself resolutely to finish *Shirley*, as a means of surcease from sorrow and pain. Beginning with the twenty-fourth chapter, "The Valley of the Shadow of Death," she writes of Caroline Helstone's illness, the tender nursing of

145

Mrs. Pryor, and the revelation of their relationship as mother and daughter. And it is at this point in the book that May Sinclair says, "Charlotte's level strength deserts her. Ever after, she falls and soars, and falls, and soars again." A mind divided, or rather a heart divided, between life and the grave —what could one expect! Yet it is in the second part of the book that Emily emerges as an element—like wind or rain or sunlight—in the character of Shirley herself. And it is the second part, with all its faltering and inequality, its soaring and falling, that is the most stimulating and uplifting, often the most intense, due to the character of Shirley Keeldar.

Furthermore, any fluctuation in the artistic qualities of *Shirley* does not rob it of the idea, the concept, that Charlotte Brontë had for the novel. She was concerned with the heralding of a new industrial era, the coming in of the "industrial age," in which the use of machinery was already beginning to have its effect on labor. While the new inventions, and their effect on the working man, served as Charlotte's protagonist in the industrial drama just commencing, she also introduced the political crisis, brought about by the Napoleonic war, which had caused the government to prohibit the products of British mills from being sold to neutral countries. And in *Shirley* we have Robert Moore caught on the horns of the economic dilemma thus precipitated.

Robert Moore was fighting to maintain his business solvency against political restrictions with the use of labor-saving devices; his rigid, unsympathetic attitude toward the workers, antagonistic to begin with because of his foreign extraction, made the conflict a class war as well as an economic. Into this struggle Shirley Keeldar stepped, supporting Moore's industrial investment with money of her own, at the same time reconciling her conscience by assisting the dissident working class with practical charity and human sympathy.

As can be seen, Shirley Keeldar is Charlotte's new concept of womanhood. She is drawn, not so much as a rebel against the strictures society had imposed upon her sex, as a prophecy of woman's coming equality with man in his participation in the world of affairs. The development of Shirley's character is masterfully accomplished through action and scene, a composite of the two. We get it through the wooing of Sir Philip Nunnely; the angry discussions between Shirley and her uncle when she refuses to marry Sir Philip; the diary of Louis Moore, who loves Shirley on paper until the end of the book; the walks with Caroline Helstone on the heath when Shirley talks of all earthly beauties; the conversation between the two women as they watch the workers' riot in the night:

> "They come on!" cried Shirley. "How steadily they march in! There is discipline in their ranks—I will not say there is courage; hundreds against tens are no proof of that quality; but (she dropped her voice) there is suffering and desperation amongst them—these goads will urge them forward."
> "Forwards against Robert—and they hate him. Shirley, is there much danger they will win the day?"
> "We shall see. Moore and Helstone are of earth's first blood—no bunglers—no cravens—"
> A crash—smash—shiver—stopped their whispers. A simultaneously-hurled volley of stones had saluted the broad front of the mill, and with all its windows; and now every pane of every lattice lay shattered and pounded fragments. A yell followed this demonstration—a rioters' yell—a north-of-England—a Yorkshire—a West Riding—a

West Riding-clothing-district-of-Yorkshire rioters' yell.
You never heard that sound, perhaps, reader? So much
the better for your ears—perhaps for your heart; since, if
it rends the air in hate to yourself, or to the men or principles you approve, the interests to which you wish well,
Wrath wakens to the cry of Hate: the Lion shakes his
mane, and rises to the howl of the Hyena: Caste stands
up, ireful, against Caste; and the indignant, wronged
spirit of the Middle Rank bears down in zeal and scorn
on the famished and furious mass of the Operative Class.
It is difficult to be tolerant—difficult to be just—in such
moments.

Caroline rose; Shirley put her arm round her; they
stood as still as the straight stems of two trees. That yell
was a long one, and when it ceased, the night was yet full
of the swaying and murmuring of a crowd.

"What next?" was the question of the listeners. Nothing
came yet. The mill remained mute as a mausoleum.

"He *cannot* be alone!" whispered Caroline.

"I would stake all I have, that he is as little alone as
he is alarmed," responded Shirley.

This final declaration of Shirley's under the stress of the
violence which the two girls were witnessing, is the key to
the spirit of Shirley Keeldar, reflecting that of Emily Brontë,
drawing its strength from mystical powers. For Shirley and
Caroline were speaking of a man they both loved, Caroline
with a tender devotion but with an uncomprehending innocence, Shirley with a mystic power of plumbing the human
soul; Caroline in deadly fear for Robert's life, Shirley with
courage for his soul. When she said that Robert Moore,
menaced as he was by the angry mob, was as little alone as
he was alarmed, she was stating the case for God. The magic

148

Haworth Church. *Copyright, Walter Scott.*

Roe Head School from a pencil drawing by Charlotte. *Photograph by Walter Scott. Copyright, The Brontë Society*

of Shirley's personality had come to burn with a steady flame under her complex and unpredictable behavior.

In *Shirley*, Charlotte Brontë leaves the parsonage and the classroom and goes out into the world of business, into the affairs of men. Many men play important roles in Shirley's life, in her public life as well as her private life. She is surrounded by men; and she holds her own among them, from the standpoint both of intellect and of integrity. It seems to me to be one of the mysterious aspects of Charlotte's genius that at so young an age, and living the secluded and penurious life of a minister's daughter, she could give us the men she has drawn in *Shirley*. All of them are recognizably flesh and blood, no mere figments of a girl's imagination. Her men are sturdy and strong, with all the virtues and faults of human beings. They do not stand on pedestals. She skillfully satirizes the insipid weakness of the curates, Messrs. Malone, Sweeting, and Donne; and yet the rector, Mathew Helstone, is a cleric of determined political principles, a Tory, a skeptic where women are concerned (and particularly where his niece Shirley is concerned), who fearlessly and manfully defends the law against the rioters. Robert Moore, Hiram Yorke, Joe Scott, Mr. Sykes, even the hypocritical dissenters, Moses Barraclough and Michael Hartley, are all realities. In Hiram Yorke, Charlotte has been said to have created her most powerful male character. A native of Yorkshire, with cultural refinements acquired from foreign travel and wide associations, with an uncompromising yet understanding attitude toward human frailty, Hiram Yorke is done with a power and unerring penetration that makes him memorable in the roster of Charlotte's creations. Hiram's racy Yorkshire dialect, expressing such wise insight, is done with a true ear for the tang of originality of expression. The wisdom may be harsh,

149

but it is lit by such a spirit of sweet intelligence and faith as to soften the sting. Although his part in the story is comparatively minor, he gives the impression of a major force, outweighing the rigid financial obsessions of Robert Moore, or the ineffectual, though noble, aspirations of his brother, Louis Moore. And, speaking of Louis Moore, it must have been in a moment of impulse that Charlotte chose him, of them all, to become Shirley's husband. Perhaps because, having made the problems of society, rather than romance, her "leading men," she was not so deeply concerned with Shirley's affairs of the heart as she had been with Jane's and Lucy's. She could thus give Shirley away to any one of several men, provided they were *worthy* aspirants.

Shirley's relation to Caroline is extremely interesting, in view of the relationship of Emily, Anne, and Charlotte. Caroline might well have been Anne, as Shirley was Emily. Shirley sees with patient and loving understanding, with compassionate sympathy, the gnawing hunger of love for Robert Moore that is eating Caroline's heart away. She herself feels irresistibly drawn into the flame of Robert Moore's dynamic personality, his vigor and drive, yet she doesn't allow the faintest intimation of her own feelings to shadow her friendship for Caroline. Caroline sinks under the burden of her unrequited love, and becomes very ill. Shirley sends her own governess-companion, the mysterious Mrs. Pryor, to nurse Caroline; it is then that Caroline discovers that Mrs. Pryor is her mother. For all the danger invited by such a reunion for one of Charlotte's lapses into sentimentality, this is one of the tenderest and most moving scenes in any of the novels.

What makes Shirley endearing, and a triumph of Charlotte's imagination, is that she is a symbol of the unity between the human spirit and the profound realities of nature. Shirley, like Emily, knew how to break through the façade of man's creation to worship at the altars of those truths. In *Shirley,* Charlotte Brontë used to greatest advantage her familiarity with the Yorkshire background. The first part of *The Professor,* and certain parts of *Jane Eyre,* find her painting the scene she knew by heart, but in neither of these novels does she weave such a pattern of natural and psychological details, giving the temper and substance of a place and its people, as she does in *Shirley.* In Shirley her love of the Haworth country is transfigured by the spirit of Emily and takes on a new significance. In one incomparable passage, which May Sinclair has called a "great prose hymn," Shirley utters a paean of adoration of Earth that is incomparable in its ecstatic fervor:

"How pleasant and calm it is!" said Caroline.
"And how hot it will be in the church!" responded Shirley: "and what a dreary long speech Dr. Boultby will make! and how the curates will hammer over their prepared orations! For my part, I would rather not enter."
"But uncle will be angry, if he observes our absence."
"I will bear the brunt of his wrath: he will not devour me. I shall be sorry to miss his pungent speech. I know it will be all sense for the Church, and all Causticity for Schism: he'll not forget the battle of Royd-lane. I shall be sorry also to deprive you of Mr. Hall's sincere friendly homily, with its racy Yorkshireisms; but here I must stay. The gray church and grayer tombs look divine with this crimson gleam on them. Nature is now at her evening prayers: she is kneeling before those red hills. I see her prostrate on the great steps of her altar, praying for a fair night for mariners at sea, for travellers in the deserts,

151

for lambs on moors, and unfledged birds in woods. Caroline, I see her! and I will tell you what she is like: she is like what Eve was when she and Adam stood alone on earth."

"And that is not Milton's Eve, Shirley."

"Milton's Eve! Milton's Eve! I repeat. No, by the pure Mother of God, she is not! Cary, we are alone: we may speak what we think. Milton was great; but was he good? His brain was right: how was his heart? He saw heaven: he looked down on hell. He saw Satan, and Sin his daughter, and Death their horrible off-spring. Angels serried before him their battalions: the long lines of adamantine shields flashed back on his blind eyeballs the unutterable splendour of heaven. Devils gathered their legions in his sight: their dim, discrowned, and tarnished armies passed rank and file before him. Milton tried to see the first woman; but, Cary, he saw her not!"

"You are bold to say so, Shirley."

"Not more bold than faithful. It was his cook that he saw; or it was Mrs. Gill, as I have seen her, making custards, in the heat of summer, in the cool dairy, with rose-trees and nasturtiums about the latticed window, preparing a cold collation for the rectors,—preserves, and 'dulcent creams'—puzzled

What choice to choose for delicacy best;
What order so contrived as not to mix
Tastes, not well-joinéd, inelegant; but bring
Taste after taste, upheld with kindliest change."

"All very well too, Shirley."

"I would beg to remind him that the first men of the earth were Titans, and that Eve was their mother: from her sprang Saturn, Hyperion, Oceanus: she bore Prometheus—"

152

"Pagan that you are; what does that signify?"

"I say, there were giants on the earth in those days: giants that strove to scale heaven. The first woman's breast that heaved with life on this world yielded the daring which could contend with Omnipotence: the strength which could bear a thousand years of bondage,—the vitality which could feed that vulture death through uncounted ages,—the unexhausted life and uncorrupted excellence, sisters to immortality, which, after milleniums of crimes, struggles, and woes, could conceive and bring forth a Messiah. The First woman was heaven-born: vast was the heart whence gushed the well-spring of the blood of nations; and grand the undegenerate head where rested the consort-crown of creation."

"She coveted an apple, and was cheated by a snake; but you have got such a hash of Scripture and mythology into your head that there is no making any sense of you. You have not yet told me what you saw kneeling on those hills."

"I saw—I now see—a woman-Titan: her robe of blue air spreads to the outskirts of the heath, where yonder flock is grazing; a veil white as an avalanche sweeps from her head to her feet, and arabesques of lightning flame on its borders. Under her breast I see her zone, purple like that horizon: through its blush shines the star of evening. Her steady eyes I cannot picture; they are clear—they are as deep as lakes—they are lifted and full of worship—they tremble with the softness of love and the lustre of prayer. Her forehead has the expanse of a cloud, and is paler than the early moon, risen long before the dark gathers: she reclines her bosom on the ridge of Stilbro' Moor; her mighty hands are joined beneath it. So kneeling, face to face she speaks with God. That Eve is Jehovah's daughter, as Adam was his son."

153

"She is very vague and visionary! Come, Shirley, we ought to go into church."

"Caroline, I will not: I will stay out here with my mother Eve, in these days called Nature. I love her— undying, mighty being! Heaven may have faded from her brow when she fell in paradise; but all that is glorious on earth shines there still. She is taking me to her bosom, and showing me her heart. Hush, Caroline! you will see her and feel as I do, if we are both silent."

It is therefore little wonder that Shirley Keeldar, with her freed spirit that went straight to God and asked no "middle man," should have stirred the wonder and admiration of the Yorkshire folk, from the hardheaded business executive, Robert Moore, to the simple laborer, William Farren, touching their lives with a beauty they knew not of. The insight that Shirley possessed, and that Caroline called visionary, was supported by a creed, call it pagan if you will. It had the power to magnetize men to action, though it needed no doctrinal exhortation to work its effect. It was accomplished by a smile, a word, a service rendered, starlighted with some divine fire of the senses.

"I have spent the afternoon and evening at Fieldhead," Louis Moore writes in his diary. "Some hours ago she passed me, coming down the oak-staircase-window, looking at the frost-bright constellations. How closely she glided against the bannisters! How shyly shone her large eyes upon me! How evanescent, fugitive, fitful, she looked—slim and swift as a Northern Streamer! I followed her into the drawing-room. Mrs. Pryor and Caroline Helstone were both there. She summoned me to bear her company for awhile. In her evening dress; with her long hair flowing full and wavy; with her noiseless step, her pale cheek, her eye full of night and

154

lightening, she looked, I thought, spirit-like—a thing made of an element—the child of a breeze and a flame—the daughter of ray and raindrop—a thing never to be overtaken, arrested, fixed . . . Once I only *saw* her beauty, now I *feel* it."

That was the secret of Shirley's power over all who knew her. They saw her great external beauty, her charm of manner, but as these became more and more familiar, they began to *feel* her innate qualities, and suddenly found themselves in labyrinths of emotion from which they had no desire to extricate themselves. Clearly it was the spirit of Emily Brontë, immortalized by her sister Charlotte Brontë, that had led them into her inner sanctum.

*Chapter* XVII   VILLETTE

CRITICAL opinion seems to be agreed that *Villette* is Charlotte Brontë's masterpiece. She poured into this novel, her fourth and last to be completed before her own untimely death at the age of thirty-nine, all the poetry and music of love as her passionately poetic nature conceived love to be. (She began a fifth novel, entitled *Emma*, that was destined to remain a fragment.) Her heroine, Lucy Snowe, is among the finest creations in English literature, and she is made so out of the depths of Charlotte's own heart. A glowing ardor holds the story to a high pitch of emotional excitement. *Villette* does not "soar and fall, soar, and fall again," as does *Shirley* in its later pages. It rises quickly to a level that is sustained throughout. No psychological or political implications confuse the issue, as in *Jane Eyre* and *Shirley*, and, whereas many of the incidents could have weighted the book with tragedy, it is rescued by the saving grace of a delicate and exquisite comedy, which gives the story a certain wistful pathos. The extraordinarily adept mingling of comedy and pathos is a constant source of delight to the reader. "It is this utter purity," Miss Sinclair says, "this transparent simplicity, that makes *Villette* great." One is tempted, in speaking of *Villette*, to use a cliché, and say that it was indeed written in the white heat of inspiration.

The action of *Villette* occurs within a very narrow range.

It all takes place at a girls' school in Villette (Brussels), with a few excursions in and out of the city. There is no question, nor was one obviously intended, that the school is the school Charlotte attended in Brussels in 1842 and 1843, when she and Emily were sent abroad for a few brief months of study. How much further the similarity goes has become a matter of almost legendary conjecture. As in the case of Emily Dickinson, and her journey to Philadelphia, there has been endless controversy as regards what happened when Charlotte first went forth into the world. Is the story of Villette, in other words, the result of Charlotte's frustrated love for M. Heger of the Heger Pensionnat? Did she really fall in love with her teacher, or was she in love with love, or did she merely feel the first stirrings of infatuation for someone of the opposite sex whom she admired as her intellectual superior? Whatever the emotion, was it reciprocated, or frustrated, or quickly sublimated? Several things lend credence to the theory that Charlotte was deeply stirred, and that she did not conceal the fact from M. Heger. For one thing, her letters to him, after her return to England, indicate an urgent desire to receive letters in return—although the desire would appear to be for a correspondence between two minds that thought in unison rather than two hearts that beat as one. For another, Mrs. Gaskell was refused an audience by Madame Heger when she went to Brussels seeking information. But then this could have been because Madame Heger considered such a visit impertinent and uncalled for. Or perhaps, as Miss Sinclair says, "Madame did not understand these Platonic relations between English students and their French professors." Yet how Platonic was it? Charlotte herself did not want *Villette* translated into French. Backward and forward the argument swings, yes and no, no and yes. How important such a controversy becomes in the consideration of *Villette* as a work of art seems to me unimportant, even to the literary interpreter, and even though Charlotte *may* have "given herself hopelessly away." But what if she did give herself away? The love, if it was there, died a natural death from lack of response and propinquity. Why should we, a hundred years later, take its name constantly in vain? If what Charlotte felt for M. Heger awakened her romantic imagination, and gave her the key to unlock the souls of Jane and Shirley and Lucy, we should be only too thankful to M. Heger, and let Charlotte's predicament rest in peace. If, as I say, *Villette* is somewhat the fruit of experience (as why shouldn't it be, and how could it help being), it is better to let the romantic background of that experience, whether Platonic or otherwise, pass into history, and only consider the use Charlotte Brontë made of it. Far better to be grateful for the miracle wrought, somehow, somewhere, in Charlotte's soul that gave her the power to reveal love in the heart of Lucy Snowe.

We find Lucy Snowe, an orphan, living at the home of her godmother, Mrs. Bretton, in the ancient English village of Bretton. In the same household is the delightful child, Polly Home, daughter of the austere but mysterious Scotchman who turns up later, in *Villette,* as the fabulous Comte de Bassompierre. Charlotte has never lost her childhood habit of coincidental reincarnations! The Comte is one of them. And Mrs. Bretton's son, Graham, is another, since he also materializes later in the book as Dr. John. Lucy, with no security in view, leaves the Bretton home to make her way in the world, rather than be beholden. She goes up to London, where, seized by an impulse, she boards a ship for Brussels, or rather Villette. On board she becomes acquainted with a young girl, Ginevra Fanshawe, who is returning as a pupil to Madame Beck's pensionnat in Belgium. Learning that Lucy is seeking employment, Ginevra introduces her to Madame Beck, and she becomes first governess and then teacher at the school.

The years pass, until at last, suddenly, Lucy is swept into the wild, unpredictable currents of life in Villette. It all began that day she was taken desperately ill in the street and was found by Dr. John. Dr. John (the erstwhile Graham Bretton), now a doctor in Villette, takes her home to be nursed by his mother, who has, of course, followed her adored and adoring son to the Continent. From this moment Lucy becomes dramatically, and all but fatally, involved in conflicting streams of adventure, one of which has its source in the harassed and uncertain life in the Beck pensionnat; another in the affectionate and lively intercourse of the Bretton ménage, where the English of the foreign colony make themselves at home; and still a third in the lavish and fantastic apartments of the Comte de Bassompierre at the Hotel Crécy. Lucy is tossed about on these currents, and is constantly brought to the brink of disaster in her attempt to get a footing on the shifting sands of social instability in a foreign country. It is to Dr. John that she goes, as to a confessional, with every tale of woe, until she is finally so overwhelmed by hopelessness and yearning that she enters the very church she had been reared to condemn. Yet even this refuge fails her, as everything fails her, until M. Paul Emanuel, the little professor at the pensionnat, comes to her rescue with the love that passeth understanding.

The relationship of Lucy Snowe to these two men, Dr. John and M. Paul Emanuel, is the only attempt at plot to be found in *Villette*, and even that is mere skeleton. Critics have accused Charlotte of too easily transferring Lucy's love from Dr. John to M. Paul Emanuel. Yet, in my opinion, what Lucy felt for Dr. John was scarcely love at all. It was the warm affection of a young woman for an understanding masculine friend, growing out of their early associations in England, when they are thrown together, as on an island, in an alien atmosphere of suspicion and criticism. Though he is an admirable man in some ways, Dr. John's temperament is too placid to have stirred Lucy to any degree of passion. And whatever Lucy's feelings may have been toward him, Dr. John had neither the will nor the power to respond in kind. As strong a man as he appears to be outwardly, with certain appealing masculine virtues, Lucy seemed to feel that she could not depend on him in the final analysis. And her instinct did not in the end betray her, for she saw Dr. John quietly slipping into the harbor of Paulina de Bassompierre's love with no consciousness whatever that he was deserting her. On the other hand, M. Paul Emanuel, full of paradoxes as his temperament was, harbored under his tyrannical egotism a tender and kindly nature that was capable of winning Lucy's deepest admiration and respect. And it is on such a final bedrock of integrity that love is anchored. Mr. Augustine Birrell makes an admirable comparison between the two men who so deeply affected the pattern of events in which Lucy Snowe found herself emotionally tangled: "Though M. Paul may have had an actual counterfeit, the original was a long way back in Miss Brontë's life experience. It is a memory picture—hence in its mellowness, its idealization, it approaches a true creation. When we compare it with Dr. John, whose counterfeit was close at hand, we perceive the advantages of distance. M. Paul rises mysteriously from the depths of his author's mind, and brings with him tokens of what had so long been his romantic rest-ing-place, whereas the doctor, apart from Lucy Snowe's rhapsodies about him, does but bob up and down the surface like a painted cork."

Possibly the most intriguing chapter in *Villette*, certainly one that has roused most comment, is "The Long Vacation." It describes a distraught Lucy, sick at heart, wandering the streets, seeking what she could not find nor had any hope of finding, finally to be overtaken by the unaccountable impulse to seek the confessional of the church. Lucy exclaims:

That vacation! Shall I ever forget it? I think not. Madame Beck went, the first day of the holidays, to join her children at the sea-side; all the three teachers had parents or friends with whom they took refuge; every pro-fessor quitted the city; some went to Paris, some to Boue-Marine; M. Paul set forth on a pilgrimage to Rome; the house was left quite empty, but for me, a servant, and a poor deformed and imbecile pupil, a sort of cretin, whom her stepmother in a distant province would not allow to return home.

My heart almost died within me; miserable longings strained its chords. How long were the September days! How silent, how lifeless! How vast and void seemed the desolate premises! How gloomy the forsaken garden—grey now with the dust of a town-summer departed. Looking forward at the commencement of those eight weeks, I hardly knew how I was to live to the end. My spirits had been gradually sinking; now that the prop of employment was withdrawn, they went down fast. Even to look forward was not to hope: the dumb future spoke no comfort, offered no promise, gave no inducement to bear present evil in reliance on future good. A sorrowful indifference to existence often pressed on me—a despair-

161

ing resignation to reach betimes the end of all things earthly. Alas! When I had full leisure to look on life as life must be looked on by such as me, I found it but a hopeless desert; tawny sands, with no green field, no palm-tree, no well in view. The hopes which are dear to youth, which bear it up and lead it on, I knew not and dared not know. If they knocked at my heart sometimes, an inhospitable bar to admission must be inwardly drawn. When they turned away thus rejected, tears sad enough sometimes flowed; but it could not be helped: I dared not give such guests lodging. So mortally did I fear the sin and weaknes of presumption.

It is then that Lucy seeks the priest, and tells him of her desolation.

I said I was perishing for a word of advice or an accent of comfort. I had been living for some weeks quite alone; I had been ill; I had a pressure of affliction on my mind of which it would hardly any longer endure the weight. "Was it a sin, a crime?" he inquired, somewhat startled.

I assured him on this point, and, as well as I could, I showed him the mere outline of my experience.

He looked thoughtful, surprised, puzzled. "You take me unawares," he said. "I have not had such a case as yours before: ordinarily we know our routine, and are prepared; but this makes a great break in the common course of confession. I am hardly furnished with counsel fitting the circumstances."

Lucy has assured the priest that her problem involves neither sin nor crime, which would appear to rule out the possibility that she could be speaking for Charlotte, since Charlotte would certainly consider her love for M. Heger a sin, M. Heger being a married man. Whereas if she is speaking for herself, and referring to her feeling for Dr. John as a sin of "weakness and presumption," it would be natural for the priest, used to instructing those who covet their neighbors' wives, to say that her request for counsel made a great break in the common course of confession. He can do little for her, and Lucy goes forth again into streets swept with storm and chilled with the night. Fatigue and cold and misery bring her to the point of collapse, when by good fortune Dr. John finds her and carries her to his home.

As Lucy recovers consciousness she finds herself in a strange room, but it is filled with furnishings that are somehow familiar. Everything is bewildering, real and yet not real, present and yet illusory. Her predicament is symbolic of Charlotte Brontë's deepest philosophy of life. To Charlotte love in the heart of a woman is as Lucy in that room in Dr. Bretton's house: "Of all these things," says Lucy, "I could have told the peculiarities, numbered the flaws and cracks, like any clairvoyant. But where was I? Not only in what spot of the world, but in what year of our Lord? For all these objects were of past days, and of a distant country. Ten years ago I bade them good bye; since my fourteenth year they and I have never met. I gasped audibly, 'where am I?'"

She is drugged to sleep by a potion, and on waking finds Mrs. Bretton at her bedside. There is recognition, and reunion, in the course of which Lucy admits that she has known from the first that Dr. John was the Graham Bretton of those long-ago days in the English village. How pathetic is Lucy's longing for friendship—beyond friendship she seems never to have hoped—in that she could be so grateful for the acknowledged reunion with the Brettons, mother and son.

When I had said my prayers [she says], and when I was undressed and laid down, I felt that I still had friends. Friends, not professing vehement attachment, not offering the tender solace of well-matched and congenial relationships; on whom, therefore, but moderate demand of affection was to be made, of whom but moderate expectation formed. "Do not let me think of them too often, too much, too fondly," I implored: "let me not run athirst, and apply passionately to its welcome waters: let me not imagine in them a sweeter taste than earth's fountains know. Oh! would to God I may be enabled to feel enough sustained by an occasional, amicable intercourse, rare, brief, unengrossing and tranquil; quite tranquil!"

Still repeating this word, I turned to my pillow; and *still* repeating it, I steeped that pillow with tears.

But this was the turning point in Lucy Snowe's life. She had reached such depths of unhappiness that the only way out was up. Her purgation had been complete, and her spirit emerged indestructible. She could say, "A new creed became mine—a belief in happiness." This creed stood her in good stead many times thereafter. It is put to test again and again, before Lucy finds serenity in the haven of M. Paul Emanuel's loving care. It had to bear with Paulina de Bassompierre when Paulina confides in her the secret love she has bestowed on Dr. John; with Paulina's father in an attempt to reconcile him to what he considers his daughter's misplacement of her affections; with Père Salas, who misrepresents M. Paul Emanuel's "past" in order to turn her against him; with the hoax perpetrated by Ginevra Fanshawe and the Comte de Hamal; with, above all else, the long and difficult task of penetrating the shell of petty egotism covering the passionate charity of M. Paul Emanuel's soul.

M. Paul, in his turn, is the touchstone that transforms Lucy Snowe from the plain little English girl, adrift in a world of uncertainty, doubt, and despair, into the fine-tempered, sane woman, who comes to be mistress of the house in Faubourg Clotilde: "Externat de demoiselles, Numero 7, Faubourg Clotilde. Directrice, Mademoiselle Lucy Snowe." M. Paul will perhaps always remain an enigma to the students and critics of Charlotte Brontë. If Charlotte did draw on reality for the materials that go into M. Paul's character, she gave them a significance beyond that of reality. It takes a close and sympathetic scrutiny, a *study* of the finest lines Charlotte ever drew, to understand M. Paul. The understanding must come as slowly as it came to Lucy herself. For, beginning with the chapter, "Monsieur's Fête," we follow the unfolding of M. Paul's love, concealed as it has been under the eccentricities that have heretofore been deceptive, even annoying. On the day of the fête Lucy saw him being honored by his friends and by the school, and she felt a first impulse of true affection for him. She warns the reader, however, "Do not be in any hurry with kindly conclusions, or to suppose, with an over-hasty charity, that from that day M. Paul became a changed character—easy to live with, and no longer apt to flash danger and discomfort around him. No; he was naturally a little man of unreasonable moods. When overwrought, which he often was, he became acutely irritable; and, besides, his veins were dark with a livid belladonna tincture, the essence of jealousy. I do not mean merely the tender jealousy of the heart, but that sterner, narrower sentiment whose seat is in the mind."

How could it happen that such opposing dispositions as those of Lucy and M. Paul could have been eventually resolved into a single force, a single purpose? Charlotte

Brontë's genius has accomplished the feat of bringing it about. From that "narrower sentiment whose seat is in the head," a fire of passion rises up and spreads until it envelops Lucy and Paul in a single pinnacle of flame. In the transformation of Lucy and M. Paul from friends into lovers, Charlotte has revealed the mystery of the power of a woman's heart to transfigure and fuse the nature of man. She had gone a long way toward such a clarification in both *Jane Eyre* and *Shirley*, but in *Villette* she has achieved a revelation of the synthesis of the actual and the imaginary, the visible and the invisible, the present and the beyond, in human love as it is known on earth.

*Chapter* xviii   WUTHERING HEIGHTS

Emily Brontë is the most inscrutable
figure in English literature. Of the three Brontë sisters she
is the most difficult to analyze, her genius the most extraordinary and mysterious. Charlotte may have been complex and
neurotic, but she is understandable, her nature is comparatively transparent. Her experiences as a girl and as a woman
are clearly revealed in her novels. Her letters are autobiographical. Even Anne, shy and simple though she was, speaks
as though in the first person in her fiction. Agnes Grey is
Anne Brontë. But when we come to Emily we have no personal record. Charlotte supplied, and possibly destroyed,
all we will ever know about Emily in the biographical sense.
Yet the Brontë genius is most powerful, most intense, in the
poetry and prose of Emily. The secret by which she became
possessed of such power and intensity is still a secret. No one,
not even her sister, has been able to push aside the veil that
shrouds her creative impulses, to offer an explanation for the
dazzling manifestation of the tragic vision with which Emily
penetrated the human spirit. Explaining it with the one word
"genius" only brings us back to where we started, to the
question, "What is genius?" Why and when does it strike,
whom does it choose?

Whence, for instance, comes the story of *Wuthering
Heights?* Perhaps Miss Hinkley, in her study of the novel,

has given us as good an answer as any: "Emily Brontë got her ideas from the wide, primitive, half-savage little squires around Haworth. She got them from hearing, at Miss Patchett's, the story of a man who obtained a property by marrying successively a mother and daughter. She got them from tales of her Irish grandfather, who was brought up by a harsh uncle. She got them from such a book or such a magazine. . . . The genius lies in the combination."

Yes, the genius surely lies in the combination. But the combination of what? Here is such a fusion of imagination and reality, of extravagance and truth, that many a metaphor, simile, symbol has been devised to interpret that strange wild story named *Wuthering Heights*. Again it is Charlotte, the loyal and admiring sister, so brilliant in her own right, who makes a great symbol of the story. "It was," she says, "hewn in a wild workshop, with simple tools, out of homely materials. The statuary found a granite block on a solitary moor; gazing thereon he saw how from the crag might be elicited a head, savage, swart, sinister; a form moulded with at least one element of grandeur—power. He wrought with a rude chisel, and from no model but the vision of his meditations. With time and labor the crag took human shape; and there it stands colossal, dark and frowning, half-statue, half-rock; in the former sense, terrible and goblin-like; in the latter, almost beautiful, for its coloring is of mellow grey, and moorland moss clothes it; and heath, with its blooming bells and balmy fragrance, grows faithfully close to the giant's foot."

The secret of *Wuthering Heights* lies very simply in the power to bring nature and man into passionate focus. As Virginia Woolf says, when Emily wrote of thunder she made it roar, of the wind, she made it blow. The moors gave her

168

the thunder and the wind until the earth with all its mysteries became a revelation. Humanity gave her its pitiful sadness, its frustrations and anguish. Relating the two she plumbed the very depths of love and passion.

Professor Wilbur Cross declares that *Wuthering Heights* is unquestionably a novel of vengeance. Many critics share this opinion. On the other hand there are those who consider it a tale of retribution. Both points of view are essentially true. Vengeance and retribution, as Emily uses them, are symptoms of a passion that has escaped the discipline and control necessary to society. The acts of vengeance, and the inevitability of retribution, are the results of disobeying natural laws; and the inverted loves of Heathcliff and Catherine are just such a disobedience. While on earth these two were compelled to pay the penalties of vengeance, accept the punishment of retribution, redemption, in their union after death, is the ultimate answer. Emily has left us in no doubt about that meeting in eternity, for Cathy is made to say, "I am Heathcliff. He's always in my mind; not as a pleasure, any more than I am always a pleasure to myself, but as my own being. So don't talk of our separation again; it is impracticable." And Heathcliff, parting from her as she dies, cries out in a paroxysm of unrestrained yearning, "Oh, God, it is unutterable. I *cannot* live without my life. I *cannot* live without my soul."

The structure of the novel may be poor. One hardly notices, since the total impression is one of unsurpassed unity of purpose. There is no letdown after the pace is set. The faltering opening chapters suddenly run together into a single stream of forces unleashed by uncontrolled emotion: the pounding and crushing of the diabolical engine which is Heathcliff's soul, tearing and rending every relationship in

169

its path in pursuit of the pure soul of Catherine Earnshaw. By all standards of morality Heathcliff is a man of revolting greed, of bestial habits, inhuman cruelty. Yet his one supreme aspiration, enraged though it is by being thwarted, has all the constancy and force of a spiritual ideal. Heathcliff is an anomaly, as much so as the fair flower blooming from the bed of offal.

It has been stated that Emily has drawn no portraits in *Wuthering Heights,* that all her characters are abstractions. Granted that most of them are, or at least that Heathcliff and Catherine Earnshaw are the symbols of vengeance and retribution, yet it cannot be denied that several of them bear a striking resemblance to people she knew, or are a composite of people she knew, heard about, or read about. It was a facet of her genius that she could fuse the characteristics of various persons into a single *idea.* She recreated them in the terms of her own vision. She transformed realities into symbols. She worked with a magic that makes identification of the originals largely a matter for the academicians, the scholars.

It is supposed, for instance, that Mr. Joshua Taylor, father of Charlotte's school friends, Mary and Martha Taylor, was Emily's model for Heathcliff—as he certainly was Charlotte's for Mr. Rochester, Hiram Yorke, and Yorke Hunsden. Independent of mind, harsh in manner, a rebel against accepted institutions, Mr. Taylor half-frightened, half-shocked those who came in contact with him. It was said that an early disappointment in love had made him a dour man and a hard one, and this lent a certain glamour to his stern behavior. However, I personally consider that Emily owed less to Joshua Taylor, in her delineation of Heathcliff, than to Welsh, her grandfather's harsh uncle who exiled him from his home in Ahaderg. Heathcliff, like Welsh, was a strange dark-skinned waif brought into a home where he wreaked emotional havoc from start to finish. Like Welsh, Heathcliff grew up to be a cruel, conniving man, obtaining control of his benefactor's property. Between Welsh and Mr. Taylor, Emily had ample material with which to make Heathcliff a character goaded to his doom by violent obsessions and an incorrigible obstinacy.

In Catherine Earnshaw it is quite possible, as has been often suggested, that Emily was thinking of Charlotte's schoolmate in Brussels, Charlotte's Ginevra Fanshawe. But again it seems to me that Catherine, certainly in her passionate defiance, more nearly resembles Emily's own Augusta Geraldine Almeda of the Gondal epic. I also feel that in the scenes where Catherine is most vital, in sensibility and in spirit, it is Emily herself who is speaking.

The fact that, in this novel, there is a "narrator" is a clear indication that Emily is still under the spell of her childhood and adolescent writing. It was an old Brontë custom, so to speak, to have the story told by one who takes little or no part in the action concerned. In *Wuthering Heights* the custom is continued in the persons of Lockwood and Nelly Dean. It has been suggested that Lockwood bears a resemblance to Branwell, but this I cannot see. Lockwood is a mere artifice, no more. The moving story of Catherine Earnshaw's life, the malevolent influence of Heathcliff's power, has no real effect on Lockwood. They merely produce in him a half-cynical, contemptuous interest that sees him through a tedious period of convalescence in the country. He bestows neither color nor emphasis on the tale. From Nelly Dean, the old housekeeper, who was herself a part of all that happened, we get the moods, the suffering, the crises, through which the lovers passed. And in spite of her impatient and censorious attitude toward Catherine, her bitter hatred of the savage Heathcliff, she draws us irresistibly to her by voice and gesture as she talks. Emily must have realized, after the first chapters, that Lockwood was not man enough to be the narrator and so turned the task over to Nelly Dean, reducing Lockwood to a bed of illness!

This might also explain the weakness of the opening pages —indeed, it is a far more logical explanation than the one put forward by several critics, that Branwell himself wrote the first four chapters. There are said to have been witnesses who testified that Branwell read these chapters at a tavern, from sheets he pulled from his coat pocket, as his contribution to a literary evening with his boon companions. A nephew of Francis Leyland (author of a book extolling Branwell's superior capabilities and gifts), being present at this occasion, claims to have recognized the chapters when *Wuthering Heights* was published. And several Brontë authorities have gone so far as to claim that seventeen chapters of the book were the work of Branwell. Such a contention is not only absurd but easily refuted by the evidence of style and development obtaining after the fourth chapter. It therefore seems to me obvious that Emily's creative inspiration took fire as soon as she took the narration out of the hands of the dull Mr. Lockwood and put it in the hands of the colorful Nelly Dean.

In Nelly Dean she had discovered the perfect instrument for her purpose—for Nelly is obviously Tabby. And there was no single individual in Emily's life, with the possible exception of Anne, whom she knew and loved so well as Tabby, the faithful old servant of the parsonage. Nelly Dean (or Tabby) is a shrewd matron of Yorkshire heritage, above her station in intelligence, opinionated, gruff but loving to those she loves, downright prejudiced against those she doesn't. She is Catherine's confidante, and being in a continual ferment of opposition to the girl's capricious outpourings of her passion for Heathcliff, her mind and spirit and tired old body become a battleground for the conflicts of *Wuthering Heights*. Any excess of feeling was histrionics to Nelly Dean: "Catherine paused and hid her face in the folds of my gown; but I jerked it forcefully away. I was out of patience with her folly." This very attitude is what makes Nelly Dean the hub of the wheel about which revolve the dark spokes of tragedy and pain that make the story of *Wuthering Heights* so poignant.

Another character in *Wuthering Heights* whose origin is clearly indicated is that of Heathcliff's sanctimonious, hypocritical servant, Joseph. Obviously Joseph began in Emily's memories of her father's description of Gallagher; the despicable Gallagher, whose cunning malignity had terrorized the miserable boyhood of her grandfather in Ireland; the Gallagher who stood by while Welsh beat Hugh Prunty unmercifully for the misdemeanors that Gallagher had himself perpetrated; the Gallagher who quoted the Bible to prove that such punishment was ordained by the Blessed Saints. The Joseph of *Wuthering Heights,* mouthing the scriptures, is just as diabolically callous to the suffering of the boy Heathcliff at the hands of the Earnshaws, and of Hareton at the hands of Heathcliff. No doubt Yorkshire had its share of such ranters as Joseph, as offensive to an orthodox churchman as to Emily. However, it was not so much the pretensions to church dogma that Emily attacks with such contemptuous scorn. Her desire seems to have been to expose the hypocrite claiming virtues that are nonexistent in the soul of the pretender. The local dissenters of the period, if we take the character of Moses Barraclough in Charlotte's *Shirley* as an example, had some justification in their repugnance for the easy living and self-righteous preaching of the clergy, but Joseph is the personification of an evil spirit, quoting the text of Christianity while practicing the arts of the Devil incarnate.

The house Wuthering Heights stood on the summit of Haworth Hill, and was once a house of fine proportions, built by a Hareton Earnshaw in the sixteenth century. All its early grandeur has been erased by time and weather, the rise and fall of many generations, and at the opening of Emily's story has become no more than an ill-conditioned farmhouse, reduced by the poverty and shiftlessness of Hindley Earnshaw. It is in such condition that Lockwood finds it when he calls on Heathcliff, having come down from London and rented Thrushcross Grange, former home of the Lintons, now Heathcliff's, for a few months' rest. And the temper of the story is immediately set by the night of horror and mystery which Lockwood, caught by a blizzard, is forced to spend in Heathcliff's home, occupying "the unused chamber," the "haunted" chamber, where Catherine Earnshaw's ghost terrifies him to such a point that he rouses Heathcliff with his cries for help.

Heathcliff stood near the entrance, in his shirt and trousers: with a candle dripping over his fingers, and his face as white as the wall behind him. The first creak of the oak startled him like an electric shock! the light leaped from his hold to a distance of some feet, and his agitation was so extreme, that he could hardly pick it up.

"It is only your guest, sir," I called out, desirous to spare him the humiliation of exposing his cowardice further. "I had the misfortune to scream in my sleep, owing to a frightful nightmare. I'm sorry I disturbed you."

"Oh, God confound you, Mr. Lockwood! I wish you were at the——" commenced my host, setting the candle on a chair, because he found it impossible to hold it steady. "And who showed you up into this room?" he continued, crushing his nails into his palms, and grinding his teeth to subdue the maxillary convulsions. "Who was it? I've a good mind to turn them out of the house this moment!"

"It was your servant, Zillah," I replied, flinging myself on to the floor, and rapidly resuming my garments. "I should not care if you did, Mr. Heathcliff; she richly deserves it. I suppose that she wanted to get another proof that the place was haunted, at my expense. Well, it is—swarming with ghosts and goblins! You have reason in shutting it up, I assure you. No one will thank you for a doze in such a den!"

"What do you mean?" asked Heathcliff "and what are you doing? Lie down and finish out the night, since you are here; but, for Heaven's sake! don't repeat that horrid noise; nothing could excuse it, unless you were having your throat cut!"

"If the little fiend had got in at the window, she probably would have strangled me!" I returned. "I'm not going to endure the persecutions of your hospitable ancestors again. Was not the Reverend Jabes Branderham akin to you on the mother's side? And that minx, Catherine Linton, or Earnshaw, or however she was called—she must have been a changeling—wicked little soul! She told me she had been walking the earth those twenty years: a just punishment for her mortal transgressions, I've no doubt!"

Scarcely were these words uttered, when I recollected

175

the association of Heathcliff's with Catherine's name in the book, which had completely slipped from my memory, till thus awakened. I blushed at my inconsideration; but, without showing further consciousness of the offence, I hastened to add—"The truth is, sir, I passed the first part of the night in"—Here I stopped afresh—I was about to say "perusing those old volumes," then it would have revealed my knowledge of their written, as well as their printed contents: so, correcting myself, I went on, "in spelling over the name scratched on that window-ledge. A monotonous occupation, calculated to set me asleep, like counting, or"—

"What can you mean talking in this way to me?" thundered Heathcliff with savage vehemence. "How—how dare you, under my roof?—God! he's mad to speak so!" And he struck his forehead with rage.

I did not know whether to resent this language or pursue my explanation; but he seemed so powerfully affected that I took pity and proceeded with my dreams; affirming I had never heard the appellation of "Catherine Linton" before, but reading it often over produced an impression which personified itself when I had no longer my imagination under control. Heathcliff gradually fell back into the shelter of the bed, as I spoke; finally sitting down almost concealed behind it. I guessed, however, by his irregular and intercepted breathing, that he struggled to vanquish an excess of violent emotion. Not liking to show him that I had heard the conflict, I continued my toilette rather noisily, looked at my watch, and soliloquised on the length of the night: "Not three o'clock yet! I could have taken oath it had been six. Time stagnates here: we must surely have retired to rest at eight!"

"Always at nine in winter, and rise at four," said my host, suppressing a groan: and, as I fancied by the motion of his arm's shadow, dashing a tear from his eyes. "Mr. Lockwood," he added, "you may go into my room: you'll only be in the way, coming downstairs so early; and your childish outcry has sent sleep to the devil for me."

"And for me, too," I replied. "I'll walk in the yard till daylight, and then I'll be off; and you need not dread a repetition of my intrusion. I'm now quite cured of seeking pleasure in society, be it country or town. A sensible man ought to find sufficient company in himself."

"Delightful company!" muttered Heathcliff. "Take the candle, and go where you please. I shall join you directly. Keep out of the yard, though, the dogs are unchained; and the house—June mounts sentinel there, and—nay, you can only ramble about the steps and passages. But, away with you! I'll come in two minutes!"

I obeyed, so far as to quit the chamber; when, ignorant where the narrow lobbies led, I stood still, and was witness, involuntarily, to a piece of superstition on the part of my landlord, which belied, oddly, his apparent sense. He got on to the bed, and wrenched open the lattice, bursting, as he pulled at it, into an uncontrollable passion of tears. "Come in! come in!" he sobbed. "Cathy, do come. Oh do—once more!" The spectre showed a spectre's ordinary caprice: it gave no sign of being; but the snow and wind whirled wildly through, even reaching my station, and blowing out the light.

There was such an anguish in the gush of grief that accompanied this raving, that my compassion made me overlook its folly, and I drew off, half angry to have listened at all, and vexed at having related my ridiculous nightmare, since it produced that agony; though why, was beyond my comprehension. I descended cautiously to the lower regions, and landed in the back kitchen, where a gleam of fire, raked compactly together, enabled

177

me to rekindle my candle. Nothing was stirring except a brindled, grey cat, which crept from the ashes, and saluted me with a querulous mew.

Lockwood's curiosity is naturally aroused, to say the least! He cannot rest until he learns the story behind the reappearance of Catherine Earnshaw, or is it Catherine Linton? And the story of Wuthering Heights now begins, at the point where Heathcliff, a "little dark thing, harbored by a good man to his bane," is brought home by the master and set down in the kitchen at Wuthering Heights. The squire soon displays an affection for this odd creature far exceeding his love for his own children. His son, Hindley, comes to hate the newcomer with a passionate and jealous fury, and Heathcliff passes a wretched childhood persecuted by his foster brother. Although Mrs. Earnshaw is often a witness to her son's cruelty, she never interferes in behalf of her husband's strange protégé. Thus wife is set against husband, father against son.

But Heathcliff finds solace in the friendship of little Catherine, Hindley's younger sister. Catherine is a lively temperamental child, with an affectionate nature. Her heart is touched by the unhappy, brooding boy, and she attaches herself to him as his only comforter, and companion-in-arms against the whole wide world. " 'The greatest punishment we could invent for her,' " Nelly Dean tells Mr. Lockwood, " 'was to keep her separate from Heathcliff. . . . Certainly she had ways with her such as I never saw a child take up before; and she put all of us past our patience fifty times and oftener in a day; till the hour she came downstairs till the hour she went to bed, we hadn't a minute's security that she wouldn't be in mischief. Her spirits were always at high-water mark, her tongue always going—singing, laughing, and plaguing everyone who would not do the same. A wild, wicked slip she was; but she had the bonniest eye, the sweetest smile, and the lightest foot in the parish. And after all I believe she meant no harm; for, when once she made you cry in good earnest, it seldom happened that she wouldn't keep you company, and oblige you to be quiet that you might comfort her. In play she liked exceedingly to act the little mistress, using her hands freely and commanding her companions.'"

Here, in their childhood together, their sharing of confidences, their combined forces against trouble, the trouble shared, love had its roots. They loved before they knew what love meant, what it would mean to *them*. So that tragedy struck before they were ready to guard against it. For it was when Catherine fell in love, or thought she had fallen in love, with Edgar Linton, that the fuse was lit for all the agony that was bound to follow. Already, Heathcliff and Catherine, had they but realized it, were inextricably and inexorably united. Catherine's marriage to Linton actually tore their souls asunder as surely as if they had been one soul. Catherine found that out too late.

Accident had thrown Catherine into the path of the Linton family at Thrushcross Grange, the fine mansion across the moors where "the gentle-folk" lived. Coming to know the Lintons, being flattered and loved by them, was her undoing. When she returned to Wuthering Heights, after several weeks in the Linton home, she was already a young lady seeing everything about her, including Heathcliff, in a new light.

Cathy [said Nelly Dean, telling Lockwood of this homecoming], catching a glimpse of her friend (Heathcliff) in his concealment, flew to embrace him; she bestowed seven or eight kisses on his cheek within the second, and then stopped, and drawing back burst into a laugh, exclaiming, "why, how very black and cross you look! and how—how funny and grim! But that's because I'm used to Edgar and Isabella Linton. Well, Heathcliff, have you forgotten me?" But the boy made no responsive move to Catherine's effusive greeting and was admonished by Hindley to shake hands, condescendingly assuring him that "once in a way, that is permitted!"

"I shall not," replied Heathcliff. "I shall not stand to be laughed at. I shall not bear it." After saying this he tried to escape, but Cathy, seizing him, explained, "I did not mean to laugh at you," she said, "I could not hinder myself. Heathcliff, shake hands at least. What are you sulky for? It is only that you looked odd. If you wash your face and brush your hair, it will be all right; but you are so dirty."

From this moment such fair currents as there had been in the lives of these two were lost in wild waters, in a stormy sea. What happiness Heathcliff had known as Cathy's playmate died with her laughter, while his love for her, instead of being weakened, went on to float on a tide of evil and vengeance. Everything that happened, from this day on, nourished his desire to destroy himself if by so doing he could destroy Catherine.

Since the death of the squire, some time previously, Hindley had increased his maltreatment of Heathcliff. But now Hindley's wife, to whom he was deeply attached, died following the birth of a son, and Hindley took out his grief in excessive drinking, gambling, and debauchery, eventually becoming an easy prey to Heathcliff's plans for vengeance on

M. Constantin Heger. *Photograph by Walter Scott. Copyright, The Brontë Society*

Emily's desk and lamp, with a letter from the publishers addressed to Currer Bell. *Photograph by Walter Scott. Copyright, The Brontë Society.*

Emily's sofa, on which she died. *Photograph by Walter Scott. Copyright, The Brontë Society.*

the entire family. He sank to a condition of degradation that put him at the mercy of one who had been, so shortly before, the victim of his own hatred. At about the same time Edgar Linton began his courtship of Catherine, inspiring in her a new ambition for the refinements of wealth, making her captious and petulant where Heathcliff was concerned, particularly since she had begun to be aware of Heathcliff's passion for her, and to realize that she was bound to Heathcliff by a bond no will or fate could break. She confessed to Nelly, "I've no more business to marry Edgar Linton than I have to be in heaven; and if the wicked man in there [meaning Hindley] had not brought Heathcliff so low, I shouldn't have thought of it. It would degrade me to marry Heathcliff now; so he shall never know how I love him: and that, not because he's handsome, Nelly, but because he's more myself than I am. Whatever our souls are made of, his and mine are the same; and Linton's is as different as a moonbeam from lightning, or frost from fire." Heathcliff, sitting noiselessly on a bench out of view, heard her say it, and stole away, but not so quietly but that Catherine was suspicious. " 'Oh,' she whispered, 'he couldn't overhear me at the door! Give me Hareton [Hindley's baby son], while you get supper, and when it is ready ask me to sup with you. I want to cheat my uncomfortable conscience, and be convinced that Heathcliff has no notion of these things. He has not, has he? He does not know what being in love is?' "

So Cathy married Edgar Linton and Heathcliff disappeared from Wuthering Heights, only to return in three years' time to make a tragic shambles of all their lives. "He had grown," said Nelly Dean, "into a tall, athletic, well-formed man; beside whom my master seemed quite slender and youth-like. His upright carriage suggested the idea of his having been in the army. His countenance was much older in expression and decision of feature than Mr. Linton's; it looked intelligent, and retained no marks of former degradation. A half-civilized ferocity lurked yet in the depressed brows and eyes full of black fire, but it was subdued; and his manner was quite dignified; quite divested of roughness, though too stern for grace. My master's surprise equalled or exceeded mine: he remained for a minute at a loss how to address the ploughboy, as he had called him."

With the reappearance of Heathcliff, Emily ignites a flame of passion that consumes everything in its course. The dissolute Hindley falls an easy prey to his hands. What Hindley had been to him as a boy, tormentor and brutalizer, he is now to Hindley's son, Hareton. He seizes the property of Wuthering Heights through mortgage foreclosures. And all the while his love for Cathy, and hers for him, is mounting to a new crescendo of burning frenzy. He cannot forgive her for marrying Edgar Linton, he could curse her forever. Yet he is more fiendishly delighted at seeing her despair and suffering than tortured with grief at his own loss. His satisfactions are sadistic. He takes delight in degrading Hareton Earnshaw with treatment more inhuman than had ever been applied to himself. But the destinies that overtake these people—the disillusioned, brow-beaten Isabella Linton, with her sordid death in London; Hindley Earnshaw, and his ruin and degraded end; Edgar Linton, and his aching, helpless endurance of his shattered love—are no more tragic than the destiny that is in store for Catherine and Heathcliff. Never had two people whose passion for each other transcended every human obstacle been so cruel to one another. Never had two people, so exultant in the ecstasy of love, been so walled around with the darkest miseries of mortal flesh. The climax to the unutterable beauty and despairing sorrow of this love is given in a chapter in which angels and demons compete to be heard above the howl of winds on the Yorkshire moors. As Catherine, expecting a child, lies desperately ill, Heathcliff writes, by way of Nelly, asking permission to see her; and on a Sunday morning, in early spring, as the Gimmerton chapel bells are calling the people to worship, the crisis of Emily Brontë's powerful novel is enacted. Let Nelly Dean tell it in her own words:

There was a startled and a troubled gleam of recollection, and a struggle to arrange her ideas. She lifted the letter, and seemed to peruse it; and when she came to the signature she sighed; yet still I found she had not gathered its import, for, upon my desiring to hear her reply, she merely pointed to the name, and gazed at me with mournful and questioning eagerness.

"Well, he wishes to see you," said I, guessing her need of an interpreter. "He's in the garden by this time, and impatient to know what answer I shall bring."

As I spoke, I observed a large dog lying on the grass beneath raise its ears as if about to bark, and then smoothing them back, announce, by a way of the tail, that some one approached whom it did not consider a stranger. Mrs. Linton bent forward, and listened breathlessly. The minute after a step traversed the hall; the open house was too tempting for Heathcliff to resist walking in: most likely he supposed that I was inclined to shirk my promise and so resolved to trust to his own audacity. With straining eagerness Catherine gazed towards the entrance of her chamber. He did not hit the right room directly, she motioned me to admit him, but he found it out ere I could reach the door, and in a stride or two was at her side, and had her in his arms.

183

He neither spoke nor loosed his hold for some five minutes, during which period he bestowed more kisses than ever he gave in his life before, I dare say: but then my mistress had kissed him first, and I plainly saw that he could hardly bear, for downright agony, to look into her face! The same conviction had stricken him as me, from the instant he beheld her, that there was no prospect of recovery there—she was fated, sure to die.

"Oh, Cathy! Oh, my life! how can I bear it?" was the first sentence he uttered, in a tone that did not seek to disguise his despair. And he stared at her so earnestly that I thought the very intensity of his gaze would bring tears into his eyes; but they burned with anguish: they did not melt.

"What now?" said Catherine, leaning back, and returning his look with a suddenly clouded brow: her humour was a mere vane for constantly varying caprices. "You and Edgar have broken my heart, Heathcliff! And you both come to bewail the deed to me, as if *you* were the people to be pitied! I shall not pity you, not I. You have killed me—and thriven on it, I think. How strong you are! How many years do you mean to live after I am gone?"

Heathcliff had knelt on one knee to embrace her; he attempted to rise, but she seized his hair, and kept him down.

"I wish I could hold you," she continued bitterly, "till we were both dead! I shouldn't care what you suffered. I care nothing for your sufferings. Why shouldn't you suffer? I do! Will you forget me? Will you be happy when I am in the earth? Will you say twenty years hence, 'That's the grave of Catherine Earnshaw. I loved her long ago, and was wretched to lose her; but it is past. I've loved many others since; my children are dearer to me

184

than she was; and at death, I shall not rejoice that I am going to her; I shall be sorry that I must leave them!' Will you say so, Heathcliff?"

"Don't torture me till I am as mad as you yourself," cried he, wrenching his head free, and grinding his teeth.

The two, to a cool spectator, made a strange and fearful picture. Well might Catherine deem that heaven would be a land of exile to her, unless with her mortal body she cast away her moral character also. Her present countenance had a wild vindictiveness in its white cheek, and a bloodless lip and scintillating eye; and she retained in her close fingers a portion of the locks she had been grasping. As to her companion, while raising himself on one hand, he had taken her arm with the other; and so inadequate was his stock of gentleness to the requirements of her condition, that on his letting go I saw four distinct impressions left blue in the colorless skin.

"Are you possessed with a devil," he pursued savagely, "to talk to me in that manner when you are dying? Do you reflect that all those words will be branded on my memory, and eating deeper eternally after you have left me? You know you lie to say I have killed you: and, Catherine, you know that I could as soon forget you as my existence! Is it not sufficient for your infernal selfishness, that while you are at peace I shall writhe in the torments of hell?"

"I shall not be at peace," moaned Catherine, recalled to a sense of physical weakness by the violent, unequal throbbing of her heart, which beat visibly and audibly under this excess of agitation. She said nothing further till the paroxysm was over; then she continued more kindly—

"I'm not wishing you greater torment than I have, Heathcliff. I only wish us never to be parted: and should

185

a word of mine distress you hereafter, think I feel the same distress underground, and for my own sake, forgive me! Come here and kneel down again! You never harmed me in your life. Nay, if you nurse anger, that will be worse to remember than my harsh words! Won't you come here again? Do!"

Heathcliff went to the back of her chair, and leant over, but not so far as to let her see his face, which was livid with emotion. She bent round to look at him: he would not permit it: turning abruptly, he walked to the fireplace, where he stood, silent, with his back towards us. Mrs. Linton's glance followed him suspiciously: every moment woke a new sentiment in her. After a pause and a prolonged gaze, she resumed; addressing me in accents of indignant disappointment,

"Oh, you see, Nelly, he would not relent a moment to keep me out of the grave. *That* is how I'm loved! Well, never mind. That is not my Heathcliff. I shall love mine yet; and take him with me; he's in my soul. And," she added musingly, "the thing that irks me most is this shattered prison, after all. I'm tired of being enclosed here. I'm wearying to escape into that glorious world, and to be always there: not seeing it dimly through tears, and yearning for it through the walls of an aching heart; but really with it, and in it. Nelly you think you are better and more fortunate than I; in full health and strength: you are sorry for me—very soon that will be altered. I shall be sorry for *you*. I shall be incomparably beyond and above you all. I *wonder* he won't be near me!" She went on to herself. "I thought he wished it. Heathcliff, dear! you should not be sullen now. Do come to me, Heathcliff."

In her eagerness she rose and supported herself on the arm of the chair. At that earnest appeal he turned to her,

186

looking absolutely desperate. His eyes, wide and wet, at last flashed fiercely on her; his breast heaved convulsively. An instant they held asunder, and then how they met I hardly saw, but Catherine made a spring, and he caught her, and they were locked in an embrace from which I thought my mistress would never be released alive: in fact, to my eyes, she seemed directly insensible. He flung himself into the nearest seat, and on my approaching hurriedly to ascertain if she had fainted, he gnashed at me, and foamed like a mad dog, and gathered her to him with greedy jealousy. I did not feel as if I was in the company of a creature of my own species: it appeared that he would not understand, though I spoke to him; so I stood off and held my tongue in great perplexity.

A movement of Catherine's relieved me a little presently: she put her hand to clasp his neck, and bring her cheek to his as he held her; while he, in return, covering her with frantic caresses, said wildly—

"You teach me now how cruel you've been—cruel and false. *Why* did you despise me? *Why* did you betray your own heart, Cathy? I have not one word of comfort. You deserve this. You have killed yourself. Yes, you may kiss me, and cry; and wring out my kisses and tears: they'll blight you—they'll damn you. You loved me—then what right had you to leave me? What right—answer me—for the poor fancy you felt for Linton? Because misery and degradation, and death, and nothing that God or Satan could inflict would have parted us, *you*, of your own will, did it. I have not broken your heart—you have broken it; and in breaking it, you have broken mine. So much the worse for me, that I am strong. Do I want to live? What kind of living will it be when you—oh, God! would you like to live with your soul in the grave?"

"Let me alone. Let me alone," sobbed Catherine. "If I

have done wrong, I'm dying for it. It is enough! You left me too: but I won't upbraid you! I forgive you. Forgive me!"

"It is hard to forgive, and to look at those eyes, and feel those wasted hands," he answered. "Kiss me again; and don't let me see your eyes! I forgive what you have done to me. I love *my* murderer—but yours! How can I?"

They were silent—their faces hid against each other, and washed by each other's tears. At least, I suppose the weeping was on both sides; as it seemed Heathcliff *could* weep on a great occasion like this.

I grew very uncomfortable, meanwhile; for the afternoon wore fast away, the man whom I had sent off returned from his errand, and I could distinguish, by the shine of the western sun up the valley, a concourse thickening outside Gimmerton chapel porch.

"Service is over," I announced. "My master will be here in half-an-hour!"

Heathcliff groaned a curse, and strained Catherine closer; she never moved.

Ere long I perceived a group of the servants passing up the road towards the kitchen wing. Mr. Linton was not far behind; he opened the gate himself and sauntered slowly up, probably enjoying the lovely afternoon that breathed as soft as summer.

"Now he is here," I exclaimed. "For Heaven's sake, hurry down! You'll not meet anyone on the front stairs. Do be quick; and stay among the trees till he is fairly in."

"I must go, Cathy," said Heathcliff, seeking to extricate himself from his companion's arms. "But if I live, I'll see you again before you are asleep. I won't stray five yards from your window."

"You must not go!" she answered, holding him as firmly as her strength allowed. "You shall not, I tell you."

188

"For one hour," he pleaded earnestly.

"Not for one minute," she replied.

"I *must*—Linton will be up immediately," persisted the alarmed intruder.

He would have risen, and unfixed her fingers by the act—she clung fast, grasping: there was mad resolution in her face.

"No!" she shrieked. "Oh, don't, don't go. It is the last time! Edgar will not hurt us. Heathcliff, I shall die! I shall die!"

"Damn the fool! There he is," cried Heathcliff, sinking back into his seat. "Hush, my darling! Hush, hush, Catherine! I'll stay. If he shot me so, I'd expire with a blessing on my lips."

And there they were fast again. I heard my master mounting the stairs—the cold sweat ran from my forehead: I was horrified.

"Are you going to listen to her ravings?" I said passionately. "She does not know what she says. Will you ruin her, because she has not wit to help herself? Get up! You could be free instantly. That is the most diabolical deed that ever you did. We are all done for—master, mistress, and servant."

That night Cathy's seven months child was born, and death quietly sealed her earthly anguish of body and soul. All night under the trees he waited for Nelly's promised word which he anticipated when it came:

"She's dead!" he said; "I've not waited for you to learn that. Put your handkerchief away—don't snivel before me. Damn you all! she wants none of *your* tears!"

"Yes, she's dead!" I answered. "... her sense never returned; she recognized nobody from the time you left her ... she lies with a sweet smile on her face; and her

189

latest ideas wandered back to pleasant early days. Her life closed in a gentle dream—may she wake as kindly in the other world."

"May she wake in torment!" cried Heathcliff, with frightful vehemence, stamping his foot, and groaning in a sudden paroxysm of ungovernable passion. "Why, she's a liar to the end! Where is she? Not *there*—not in heaven —not perished—where? Oh, you said you cared nothing for my sufferings! And I pray one prayer—I repeat it till my tongue stiffens—Catherine Earnshaw, may you not rest as long as I am living! You said I killed you—haunt me, then! The murdered *do* haunt their murderers, I believe. I know that ghosts have wandered on earth. Be with me always—take any form—drive me mad! Only *do* not leave me in this abyss, where I cannot find you. Oh, God! it is unutterable! I *cannot* live without my life! I *cannot* live without my soul!"

Yet Heathcliff lives. He cannot die, much as he wishes to die. No, he lives on for many years at Wuthering Heights, doing unspeakable harm to all those closely associated with him, carrying vengeance into the next generation. Realizing that poor, silly Isabella Linton has fallen in love with him, and that she will be her brother's heir, he elopes with her. She leaves him soon enough, taking her child, Linton, with her, and dies a miserable death in London. Linton is brought back to the moors by his uncle Edgar, and turned over to his father. He is a pathetic boy, ill and neurotic. Heathcliff is determined that he shall marry Catherine's daughter, young Cathy, so that he may feel a consummation denied to him and the girl's mother. But Linton dies of grief and frustration and illness before Heathcliff has his wish. And Cathy marries Hareton, Hindley's son, giving him something of the happiness he had never known; for Hareton, too had taken the brunt of Heathcliff's inverted hate. Until, at long last, all *too* long, Heathcliff himself dies, and the tale ends with two ghosts on the moors instead of one.

He solicited the society of no one more. At dusk, he went into his chamber. Through the whole night, and far into the morning, we heard him groaning and murmuring to himself. Hareton was anxious to enter; but I bade him fetch Dr. Kenneth, and he should go in and see him. When he came, and I requested admittance and tried to open the door, I found it locked; and Heathcliff bid us be damned. He was better, and would be left alone; so the doctor went away.

The following evening was very wet: indeed it poured down till day-dawn; and, as I took my morning walk round the house, I observed the master's window swinging open, and the rain driving straight in. He cannot be in bed, I thought: those showers would drench him through. He must either be up or out. But I'll make no more ado, I'll go boldly and look.

Having succeeded in obtaining entrance with another key, I ran to unclose the panels, for the chamber was vacant; quickly pushing them aside, I peeped in. Mr. Heathcliff was there—laid on his back. His eyes met mine so keen and fierce, I started; and then he seemed to smile. I could not think him dead: but his face and throat were washed with rain; the bedclothes dripped, and he was perfectly still. The lattice, flapping to and fro, had grazed one hand that rested on the sill; no blood trickled from the broken skin, and when I put my fingers to it, I could doubt no more: he was dead and stark!

*Chapter* XIX   AGNES GREY

History would appear to have granted Anne Brontë a place in literature only because she was the sister of Charlotte and Emily Brontë. She has never been really allowed to stand on her own. It is explained that if it had not been for Charlotte's loyal defense of Anne, the world would have accorded her very little notice. Even Miss Sinclair, who makes an honest effort to give Anne her due, introducing a new edition of *Agnes Grey* and *The Tenant of Wildfell Hall,* writes that "if we respect the pieties of tradition, it is right and fitting that the novels of Anne Brontë should follow *Wuthering Heights* and *Jane Eyre.* The Brontës created that tradition; they clung together; they refuse to be separated. Charlotte may be said to have thrust the words of her younger sister upon the public that had acclaimed her own with such violent enthusiasm and accepted Emily's somewhat reluctantly at her hands. And even now, in the second decade of the twentieth century, it is as if she still kept her hold on the frail Anne."

I dare say this hypothesis cannot be denied, but it actually has little bearing on the essential character of Anne's writing. Certainly *Agnes Grey* and *The Tenant of Wildfell Hall* show nothing of the genius and intensity of *Villette* or *Wuthering Heights,* but how many novels *are* comparable in that respect? And where does one find, even in Emily or Charlotte,

192

or any other contemporary novelist, such an attitude toward the social problems of the day, and of mankind on the whole, as are to be found in Anne's two novels? We cannot grant that Anne had genius, as her sisters had it, but we can assuredly say that she had great talent. And for the good of society talent, though not as powerful as genius, can sometimes be more useful. Anne's writing is often dull, to the point of boredom; as pointing a moral is sometimes extremely dull, while at the same time effective in bringing about necessary reforms in the social system and in human behavior. The moralities were what interested Anne. While her sisters kept them in the realm of abstractions, powerful only in the soul, repudiated by the flesh, inspiring yet confounding, Anne personified them, and in doing so produced types rather than characters. Her people are coat racks on which she hangs out her spiritual wares. Whereas in Charlotte and Emily the emotions are strong and ungovernable, in Anne they are muted; a gentle sensibility takes the place of desire; a strong undeviating will is in control.

Yet, with all her limitations, Anne's novels deserve better than they have received. As Miss Sinclair goes on to say, "Anne attacks her problem with a freedom and audacity before which her sisters' boldest enterprises seem cowardly and restrained.... There is nothing like these fragile repressed and tremulous women when a deed of daring is to be done. Anne does it with a naïveté, a demure insouciance, unknown to women of robust humour and the habit of unfettered speech. She is apparently unaware that she is doing it; that her behaviour is the least unusual, not to say revolutionary." And Charlotte, in a letter to Mr. Williams, tells him that "*Agnes Grey* is the mirror of the mind of the writer." The same may be said of *The Tenant of Wildfell Hall*. Anne, be-

193

cause she puts down exactly what she herself thinks, frankly and unemotionally, unconfused by the usual waywardness of characters in a novel, is more lucid than either of her sisters. There is no enigma, no paradox. The worst fault of Anne's mind and attitude is lack of humor, its most arresting virtue an intense piety which seeks to display the vanities and evils of human conduct as a warning to others. For instance, it was undoubtedly Branwell's misdeeds that inspired "the message" of *The Tenant of Wildfell Hall*. It is said that Emily and Charlotte did their best to turn Anne from her self-imposed task of making Branwell an example, but that she would not be swerved aside. She seemed to persist from a sense of duty, and succeeded in producing the most depressing and categorical story written by any woman novelist to date. More than any of them, from Fanny Burney and Ann Radcliffe to Mrs. Gaskell, she struck a blow in behalf of her sex with a boldness and firmness that was astonishing, establishing a record of defiance from which her successors were to take courage. Even Charlotte and Emily were "cowardly and restrained," as she was audacious, in making a frontal attack, for instance, on man's uncontested marital authority which so often amounted to tyranny; witness the scene, in *The Tenant of Wildfell Hall*, when Helen Huntington slams her bedroom door in the face of her reprobate husband. No; the epithets, so long applied to Anne, of sweet, pious, gentle, meek, are deceptive. She had a violent crusading spirit in her frail body, and her novels were written in that spirit.

Though *The Tenant of Wildfell Hall* is perhaps more often read today, due in some part to its arresting title, *Agnes Grey* is the better story. *Agnes Grey* is a novel of manners. There is no plot worth the mention, no situations that call for the

dramatic progression of incident or character. The book is
filled with thumbnail sketches of the people Anne knew in
and about Haworth, on the Yorkshire moors, in the Yorkshire manor houses where she worked as governess. They are
of two kinds, one enriched by trade, the other by the land.
Their foibles and vulgarities are etched against a pastel
screen of fading English tradition. They are not very lovable
people, although being described through the eyes of a governess, a vicar's daughter who is better bred and more in-
tellectually refined than her employers, has a great deal to
do with the satirical exposure of their traits. Agnes Grey does
not exactly boast of her superior taste and intelligence, but
she often betrays her feelings in a way that has caused her to
be considered a prig. Perhaps in some sense she was a prig.
Yet when one realizes the comfort and cheer she brought to
the poor old cottage woman, Nancy Brown, one cannot fail
to absolve Agnes of the unsavory implications the word may
have. Her attitude was a most natural one in view of the ob-
tuse cruelty of her employers who were continuously making
it apparent that they considered a governess an inferior being,
scarcely human, while at the same time demanding that she
set the highest standards of conduct and attainment for their
children, standards they could not themselves maintain as
parents. Anne resented their attitude with all the fierce pride
of the Brontë blood, and the emotion is one that flares into
words more than once:

> "*Dear* Miss Grey!" began Mrs. Murray, "it is the *strang-
> est* thing. I suppose you can't help it, if it's not your
> nature—but I *wonder* you can't win the confidence of
> Matilda, and make your society at *least* as agreeable to
> her as that of Robert or Joseph!" [the grooms].

"They can talk the best about the things in which she is most interested," I replied.

"Well! that is a strange confession, *however,* to come from her *governess!* Who is to form a young lady's tastes, I wonder, if the governess doesn't do it? I *have* known governesses who have so completely identified themselves with the reputation of their young ladies for elegance and propriety in mind and manners that they would *blush* to speak a word against them; and to hear the slightest blame imputed to their pupils was worse than to be censured in their own persons—and I really think it very natural, for my part."

"Do you, ma'am?"

"Yes, of course: the young lady's proficiency and elegance is of more consequence to the governess than her own, as well as to the world. If she wishes to prosper in her vocation she must devote all her energies to her business: all her ideas and all her ambition will tend to the accomplishments of that one object. When we wish to decide upon the merits of a governess, we naturally look at the young ladies she professes to have educated, and judge accordingly. The *judicious* governess knows this: she knows that, while she lives in obscurity herself, her pupils' virtues and defects will be open to every eye; and that, unless she loses sight of herself in their cultivation, she need not hope for success. You see, Miss Grey, it is just the same as any other trade or profession: they that wish to prosper must devote themselves body and soul to their calling; and if they begin to yield to indolence or self-indulgence they are speedily distanced by wiser competitors: there is little to choose between a person that ruins her pupils by neglect, and one that corrupts them by example. You will excuse my dropping these little hints; you know it all for your own good. Many ladies

196

would speak to you much more strongly; and many would
not trouble themselves to speak at all, but quietly look
out for a substitute. That, of course, would be the easiest
plan: But I know the advantages of a place like this to a
person in your situation; and I have no desire to part with
you, as I am sure you will do very well if you will only
think of these things and try to exert yourself a *little* more;
then, I am convinced, you would *soon* acquire that delicate tact which alone is wanting to give you a proper
influence over the mind of your pupil."

I was about to give the lady some idea of the fallacy of
her expectations; but she sailed away as soon as she had
concluded her speech. Having said what she wished, it
was no part of her plan to await my answer: it was my
business to hear, and not to speak.

It can be seen that the gentle and fragile Anne Brontë,
in spite of her quiet and unassuming appearance, could shoot
a pretty straight arrow, and an arrow with a barb of scorn.
The Murrays of this world should have been moved to sit
up and take notice. And when the Agnes Greys became the
Mrs. Westons of England, there could only have been a
sweeter and more wholesome respect for the individual,
whether servant or wife.

Anne had, as we know, worked as a governess herself. Both
Anne and Charlotte had "gone into service," and both knew,
at first hand, the arduous duties, the discriminatory insolence,
the contemptuous complaints, heaped on women who were
forced, by penury, to seek employment. The two girls had
borne these humiliations with the greatest patience and gentleness. Yet Anne could scarcely be expected to forego the
human need to give a vicarious vent to suppressed emotions
when it was Agnes Grey who suffered! Nor was it less than

natural that she should also permit Agnes Grey to fulfill many
of the dreams and aspirations she herself was never to see
fulfilled. It is probable that Anne had felt a romantic attachment to the curate of Haworth, Mr. Weightman, whose death
she mourned in a tender poem:

> Yes, thou art gone! and never more
>     Thy sunny smile shall gladden me;
> But I may pass the old church door,
>     And pace the floor that covers thee,
>
> May stand upon the cold, damp stone
>     And think that, frozen, lies below
> The lightest heart that I have known,
>     The kindest I shall ever know.
>
> Yet, though I cannot see thee more,
>     'Tis still a comfort to have seen;
> And though thy transient life is o'er,
>     'Tis sweet to think that thou hast been;
>
> To think a soul so near divine,
>     Within a form so angel fair,
> United to a heart like thine
>     Has gladdened once our humble sphere.

If so, she was impelled to bring Agnes Grey and the curate,
Edward Weston, to a happy ending, to the love and marriage
she was denied in life.

Agnes Grey is indeed a comedy of manners. There are
engaging conversations, piquant situations, delightfully satirical incidents, throughout the book. There is the Bloomfield
family, father and mother, and their ill-mannered children.
Having been summarily dismissed by Mrs. Bloomfield, Agnes
finds re-employment at Horton Lodge, the home of the

Murrays. There are four Murray cffspring, Rosalie, Matilda, John, and Charles. Their behavior and disposition are presented with a keen sense of detail. The girls, Rosalie and Matilda, are courted by men who are drawn with equal skill: Mr. Hatfield, the rector; and the baronets, Sir Thomas Ashby and Sir Harry Meltham. Miss Matilda is the most refractory member of the Murray establishment. She is a "veritable hoyden," cut somewhat after the pattern of Charlotte's Ginevra Fanshawe, and is a wicked trial to parent and governess alike. Agnes has to confess that, "as a moral agent, Matilda was reckless, head-strong, violent, and unamenable to reason. One proof of the deplorable state of her mind was that from her father's example she had learned to swear like a trooper." And therefore it is not surprising to detect a fear creeping into Anne's heart that she may have exposed her heroine to the dangerous influences of the people for whom she worked:

> As I could not make my companions better, I feared exceedingly that they would make me worse—would gradually bring my feelings, habits, capacities, to the level of their own; without, however, imparting to me their light-heartedness and cheerful vivacity.
>
> Already I seemed to feel my intellect deteriorating, my heart petrifying, my soul contracting; and I trembled lest my very moral perceptions should become deadened, my distinctions of right and wrong confounded, and all my better faculties be sunk, at last, beneath the baneful influence of such a mode of life. The gross vapours of earth were gathering around me, and closing in upon my inward heaven; and thus it was that Mr. Weston rose at length upon me, appearing like the morning-star in my horizon, to save me from the fear of utter darkness; and

I rejoiced that I had now a subject for contemplation that was above me, not beneath. I was glad to see that all the world was not made up of Bloomfields, Murrays, Hatfields, Ashbys, etc.; and that human excellence was not a mere dream of the imagination. When we hear a little good and no harm of a person, it is easy and pleasant to imagine more: in short, it is needless to analyse all my thoughts; but Sunday was now a day of peculiar delight to me (I was now almost broken in to the back corner in the carriage), for I liked to hear him—and I liked to see him, too; though I knew he was not handsome, or even what is called agreeable, in outward aspect: but, certainly, he was not ugly.

Anne Brontë drenches her quiet story in atmosphere, an attractive quality which came to be more and more a part of Victorian fiction, particularly among the minor novelists. She caught the moods and shades of the moors until they laid a dreamlike mantle over the people who passed along their winding roads, who entered the lowly cottages on the heath or the fine houses on the crests of the dark hills. Whether it is Mr. Weston, the curate, or Nancy Brown, the cripple, all are touched with the same magic that comes up from the bosom of the earth at sunset and sunrise, summer and winter, as nature turns on the wheel of time. The effect is indefinable, yet real, and is the element that can be traced in all the Brontës, whether Emily, Charlotte, or Anne, as the irresistible power of the moors, of the Haworth witchery, to effect its mysterious consummation.

Anne's intentions may have been, as Miss Sinclair says, beyond her capacity to realize in full. But the inability to shape a novel to a novelist's last, or to fill the shape with the elixir of genius, is often made a matter of less importance by the author's appealing sincerity, her crystal-clear motives, her gentle wit, so that the reader is led beyond the failures of style and conception and completes the image for himself. For, in a considerable measure, Anne Brontë attempted in *Agnes Grey* the very thing that Ethel Sidgewick and E. M. Delafield have achieved with such subtle and disciplined artistry nearly a hundred years later.

*Chapter* xx   THE TENANT OF WILDFELL HALL

THERE is nothing in English literature that quite resembles Anne Brontë's *The Tenant of Wildfell Hall*. It is truly a curious piece of fiction, seemingly without roots or precedent. The title suggests mystery, even horror. Before the reader has turned a page, he has already conjured up an ancestral curse, flight from justice, secret passages, dungeons, perhaps a ghost in the tower room! Actually there *is* a fugitive spirit in Wildfell Hall, for Helen Huntington has fled there to escape her husband. But Helen Huntington herself is far from being exotic or romantic. She is a creature obsessed with stern principles, intellectual prudery, moral preachings. If ever a novel was written for a purpose, to set forth certain precepts of man's behavior, it is *The Tenant of Wildfell Hall*. Anne intended that Helen should merely be the mouthpiece for lessons of piety, for chastising the wicked. As Mrs. Humphrey Ward has said, "Anne wrote *The Tenant* under the bitter mandate of conscience."

It has been asked so often, whence came the fountain of passion and power that gave the world *Wuthering Heights?* Few have asked what brought *The Tenant* from the pen of Anne Brontë. How could Anne, so gentle and good, so young and inexperienced, write convincingly of the sordid side of life? Charlotte felt moved to try to explain the paradox, but we are even baffled by her explanation. Anne's own preface

202

to the second edition of the novel is also an attempt to answer her critics, and justify herself for writing a tale of such unrelieved corruption. "I would not be understood to suppose," she writes, "that the proceedings of the unhappy scapegrace, with his few profligate companions I have introduced, are a specimen of the common practices of society—the case is an extreme one, as I trusted none would fail to perceive; but I know that such characters do exist, and if I have warned one rash youth from following in their steps, or prevented one thoughtless girl from falling into the very natural error of my heroine, the book has not been written in vain."

Anne wished to tell the truth, and hoped, as she says, that it would "convey its own moral to those who are able to receive it." It takes courage to tell such truths; it took courage to write *The Tenant of Wildfell Hall*. Anne did not possess the imaginative powers, the artistry of execution, of her sisters, but she shared one important quality with them that made them kin: an intellectual and emotional daring. She dared as completely in her representation of sin as they in theirs of passion and desire. The genius of all the Brontës was, in great part, a certain lack of inhibitions that made them fearless in the best sense of the word. Their acquaintance with the world, its conventions and restrictions, was so slight, so distant, that it had not yet taught them "diplomacy." Like children, they still saw no reason why what they knew to be the truth should not be told.

"As the story of *Agnes Grey*," Anne writes, "was accused of extravagant over-coloring in those very parts that were carefully copied from life, with a most scrupulous avoidance of all exaggeration, so, in the present work, I find myself censured for depicting *con amore* with 'a morbid love of the coarse and the brutal,' those scenes which, I venture to say, have not been more painful for the most fastidious of my critics to read than they were for me to describe. I may have gone too far; in which case I shall be careful not to trouble myself or my readers in the same way again; but when we have to do with vice, and vicious characters, I maintain that it is better to depict them as they really are than as they would wish to appear. To represent a bad thing in its least offensive light is, doubtless, the most agreeable course for a writer of fiction to pursue; but is it the most honest, or the safest?"

So we must take Anne very much at her word when she says that in both *Agnes Grey* and *The Tenant* she "carefully copied from life." She undoubtedly did. As I have intimated before, the dissolute Arthur Huntington has been universally accepted as a portrait of Branwell. It was surely the pain and anxiety caused by Branwell's defection, the gradual degradation of a brother who had been so loved and admired by his three sisters, that drove Anne to writing a horror story of moral degeneration, in the hope that it might, as she says, warn "one rash youth" from following in Branwell's footsteps. Naturally, since Branwell never married, Anne could not have depended upon him for the scenes of marital life she has drawn with such an unerring eye and ear for the inflections of domestic disharmony. Yet it is probable that in this also her sources lay in actual experience. There is reason to suppose, for instance, that she was fully aware of the unhappiness and discord in the family of Mr. C——, a clergyman in the nearby parish, whose conduct was so reprehensible that his wife was constantly seeking solace from Mr. Brontë. It is no more than natural that many of the case histories of Mr. Brontë's parishioners should have been known intimately to his daughters. Their curiosity alone would have seen to that.

While even though Patrick Brontë had become a rigid and lonely man, aloof from the normal exchange of confidences that should have been a part of such a household of motherless children, yet he must have now and then sought his daughters' advice and counsel in the course of his daily round of parish duties.

In the meanwhile, although the critics might continue to cavil as to the point at which Anne Brontë had "gone too far," *The Tenant of Wildfell Hall* was selling extremely well. Even Mr. Clement Shorter remarks that it was a great surprise to him that the book went into a second printing within the year. One hopes that this was a comfort to Anne, since, between the critics' attack and Charlotte's statement that the book was "an entire mistake," Anne had very little encouragement of any kind. What a satisfaction it would have been if she could have looked forward a half-century and known that a sound literary judgment was going to admit that *The Tenant of Wildfell Hall* had been much underrated. It would also have gladdened her to know that she was eventually to be praised for *creative skill* as well as *moral courage*, and that Miss Sinclair would one day write, "There are scenes, there are situations, in Anne's amazing novel which for sheer audacity stand alone in mid-Victorian literature, and would hold their own in the literature of revolt that followed." This courage is a fever of the spirit, a wild fire springing from the soul itself, that burns through any lack of craftsmanship in all the Brontë novels. The sisters shared it in common. It seemed to be both hereditary and contagious. It is what gives the scenes and situations of *The Tenant*, that Miss Sinclair found so amazing, much of the same pungent flavor that is to be found in *Wuthering Heights* or *Shirley*.

*The Tenant of Wildfell Hall* bears other resemblances to

*Wuthering Heights,* particularly in the manner of narration. As in *Wuthering Heights,* where the plot is unfolded by Nelly Dean's retelling of the story of Heathcliff and Catherine, so, in *The Tenant,* the narration follows the course of a diary explaining the mysterious tenant of Wildfell Hall, Helen Huntington.

It is a sordid story that the diary tells. A young girl, Helen Lawrence, brought up by an uncle and aunt, falls madly in love with a profligate young man, Arthur Huntington. Nothing can persuade her that he is as dissipated and evil as he is, or as hopeless of reform:

"'A few unprincipled mothers,'" her aunt expostulates, "'may be anxious to catch a young man of fortune without reference to his character; and thoughtless girls may be glad to win the smiles of so handsome a gentleman, without seeming to penetrate beyond the surface; but you, I trusted, were better informed than to see with their eyes, and judge with their perverted judgment.'

"'Nor do I, aunt,'" Helen Lawrence replies, "'but if I hate the sins, I love the sinner, and would do much for his salvation, even supposing your suspicions to be mainly true, which I do not and will not believe.'"

Helen becomes sadly disillusioned in the course of marriage. It is difficult to find, in the whole range of English fiction, a wife who suffered such torment at the hands of a husband so utterly reprobate. But neither can one have too much sympathy for Helen, who is portrayed as a cold, unemotional, intellectual snob. Her moral self-sufficiency tends to have the same irritating effect on the reader as on her husband. She endures her husband's abuse, the ribaldry of his drunken companions, his vile habits, with a complacency that only aggravates the condition. There is a child born of the union, the boy Arthur, and it is for his sake, to preserve him from corruption, that she finally runs away and goes into seclusion in Wildfell Hall. As Helen writes the story in her diary, there is a steady mounting crescendo of resentment and revolt against oppression, against what a woman has to put up with in a society that demands that she stay married, mistake or no mistake, and bear whatever trials her lord and master imposes upon her. A climax is finally reached when she shuts the door in her husband's face and flees the house. And yet, when Arthur Huntington is about to die, a wretchedly broken man, a coward in the face of death, Helen returns to ease his last hours with the assurance of God's mercy and forgiveness.

"How could I bear to think," she writes in her diary, "that that poor trembling soul was hurried away to lasting torment? It would drive me mad. But, thank God, I have hope—not only from the vague dependence on the possibility that penitence and pardon might have reached him at last, but from the blessed confidence that, through whatever purging fires the erring spirit may be doomed to pass—whatever fate awaits it—still it is not lost, and God, who hateth nothing that he hath made, will bless it in the end."

Here again, in these words, we have another example of the courage and revolt of Anne Brontë, the gentle Anne. To express any doubt of the inevitability of eternal damnation was heresy to the Victorian orthodoxy. And here is the daughter of Haworth parsonage saying that God does not hate, and that it would be madness to assume that he could condemn a soul to lasting torment. Just as Emily did not believe that any creed was a guarantee of salvation, so Anne rejected that most appalling religious dogma, belief in damnation. The true Brontë ferment of rebellion was at work in

Anne, and *The Tenant of Wildfell Hall* was no less a disturbing threat to the security of Victorian tradition than were the more brilliant *Jane Eyre* and *Wuthering Heights*.

It is only natural, Anne's philosophy being what it was, that both *Agnes Grey* and *The Tenant of Wildfell Hall* should end "happily ever after." In the one, the little governess, Agnes Grey, and the good rector, Edward Weston, are united in wedlock; and, in the other, Helen Huntington, after her husband's death, finds happiness with Gilbert Markham. Though much of the passion that splashes the pages of the novels of her sisters is lacking in Anne's, yet they are tinted with an emotional excitement of their own. They are not in the least dull, and they are not sentimental. There was a hard core of purpose in Anne around which the threads of her moral ideals were smoothly wound, and as she unwound them they never became knotted or tangled in her hands. Or, to use Anne's own metaphor and symbol, "since the priceless treasure too frequently hides at the bottom of a well, it needs some courage to dive for it, especially as he who does so will be likely to incur more scorn and obliquy for the mud and water into which he has ventured to plunge than thanks for the jewel he procures." Anne plunged, and procured the jewel again and again from the depths beneath her own limpid-clear nature. It is therefore only just that she should be given a small niche of her own in the Hall of Fame, not always remain tucked in beside Charlotte or Emily.

The poetic genius among the three Brontë sisters was Emily. The world has recognized this fact for the best part of a century, and that recognition has granted her a foremost place in the glorious line of English poets. All that can be claimed for Charlotte in her experience with the muse is that she never rose above the level of a competent versifier. Poetry was not her forte. But of Anne something can be said for her talent. She had a genuine, if fragile gift, in which sentiment and piety combined to produce a pleasing song. Her gentle note of reverence and devotion was imbued with a singular flame that sprung from her sincerity. This slender, but persuasive gift of song has, paradoxically, carried her name to more human hearts than the more powerful genius of her two sisters: two of her poems are included in church hymnals and sung by the faithful throughout the English-speaking world. How familiar to many who had never read or heard of *Agnes Grey* and *The Tenant of Wildfell Hall,* are the two verses that begin, "O God, if this indeed be all," and "I hope that with the brave and strong." It was quite in keeping with Anne's gentle nature that her fame and immortality should triumph in the quiet sanctuary of peace and meditation.

**Chapter XXI**    "WHERE DID YOU
GET THIS?"

*(A Footnote in the History of Anonymous)*

I HAVE retained, from the chapter on Charlotte Brontë's life, a particular incident that seems to me so interesting and dramatic that it deserves a small niche of its own in this biography. It concerns the day when Charlotte and Emily and Anne decided to reveal their true identity to publisher and public, and no longer camouflage themselves under the names of Currer, Ellis, and Acton Bell. No living soul except Mr. Brontë knew the secret of this anonymity. But the popularity of *Jane Eyre,* the critical furore over *Wuthering Heights,* had roused the literary world and the general reader to eager conjecture as to who the authors might be. Were the Bells men or women? Where did they live? What walk of society did they frequent? Were they one and the same person? Were they well-known figures in the literary world, masquerading under assumed names? *Jane Eyre,* in its handling of social problems, its insight into feminine psychology, and *Wuthering Heights,* with its stoical philosophy, its violent human passions, would seem to indicate experienced writers, wise in the ways of mankind and skilled in craftsmanship. Indeed, speculation was running high, wide, and handsome, when Charlotte decided it was time to make themselves known in their true colors. After all, she

210

had only taken the path of concealment because she felt women were handicapped, by the very reason of their sex, in the practice of any art. She had also known that *Jane Eyre* and *Wuthering Heights* were strong meat for anyone's dish, reader or critic, and that if it were known in advance that the authors were "ladies" there would be an uproar of shocked protest. So Charlotte, whose instincts were always so unerring in practical affairs, took the precaution of putting men's names to work that would have done any man credit.

A letter from the publishers, Smith, Elder, received on July 5, 1848, brought matters to a head. It arrived by post, protesting a rumor that had reached their ears concerning the acquisition of the American rights to the next work by the author of *Jane Eyre*. Another London firm appeared to be selling these rights to an American publisher, and the whole transaction was contrary to the arrangements agreed upon between the author of *Jane Eyre* and Smith, Elder. According to the letter, the affair hinted of double dealing on the part of Currer Bell. That was enough for Charlotte! She was stung to the quick by a suspicion of this nature, so completely unfounded. There was nothing to do but act immediately, and in the open. Smith, Elder must not be allowed to doubt the integrity of the Bells or the Brontës. The authors themselves must journey to London straightway and set the matter right!

It was decided that Charlotte and Anne would go, leaving Emily in charge at home. In fact, Emily was not in favor of the idea at all. The other two packed their satchels that day, and sent them by oxcart to the station at Keighly, several miles distant, where they would pick them up later as they took the night train for Leeds and London. Such a journey was quite an undertaking for two young women who had traveled so little. Charlotte and Emily had stopped off for a few hours in London, going and coming from Brussels. But for Anne it was a first visit there, and, sadly enough, would prove to be her last. The walk to Keighly, a distance of four miles from Haworth, was taken in the cool of the evening. A thunderstorm broke upon the sisters before they reached Keighly. It is significant that this should happen. The rage of the elements was in harmony with their own spirits, and they were neither afraid nor sought shelter from the storm.

The uncomfortable night ride in the coach from Leeds to London must have been a strange one, filled with thoughts of the past, anxiety for the morrow. Their spirits, as well as their bodies, could only have arrived somewhat the worse for the cramping night journey. They came into the city early Saturday morning, July 6, and went directly to the Chapter Coffee House, in Paternoster Row, where Charlotte had settled that they should stay. Mr. Brontë had taken Charlotte and Emily there for an overnight stay when he accompanied them to Brussels. The Chapter Coffee House had a past, having been a famous gathering place for critics and writers during its heyday in the early eighteenth century. Chatterton had written of it to his mother when he wanted to delude her about his well-being in London since it was the consort of famous men of letters. Now it was no more than a shabby, run-down inn, in the care of a slatternly couple, and patronized only by men. It was not the place for Charlotte and Anne to sleep, but they knew of no other. They were made as comfortable as possible in a long, low room with high windows, on the second story, where book-trade meetings had once been held. After freshening up from the night's journey, they breakfasted, and lingered a moment to decide what to do next in getting to Smith, Elder's in Cornhill.

"Villette" School in Rue d'Isabelle, Brussels. *Photograph by Walter Scott. Copyright, The Brontë Society.*

Brontë Bridge. *Copyright, Walter Scott.*

From Paternoster Row, the narrow street running north of
St. Paul's Churchyard, famed for its memories of the great
bookshops and publishing houses, but now crowded with
warehouses, it was only a short walk to Cornhill, where the
offices of Smith, Elder were located. Charlotte and Anne
emerged from the dim, dingy doorway of the Chapter Coffee
House into the business bustle and ferment of Paternoster
Row. They decided to economize by not taking a convey-
ance, though it might have been safer to rely on a driver for
directions, and made the dome of St. Paul's a guiding star in
the confusion and complexity of the innumerable crooked
streets and alleys. But St. Paul's was not always in sight.
Surely, they must have asked a stranger the way. And how
little he knew that he was directing Apollo's anointed. Two
young country women, attired in plain black homemade
gowns, one of them possessed of strange, compelling, reddish-
brown eyes, the other of a pale fragile face touched with the
loveliness of a white flower, had asked their way to Cornhill—
that was all he knew.

Perhaps a little breathless with haste and uncertainty, but
no doubt grateful that they had come thus far with no un-
toward experience, the two sisters arrived at the offices of
their publishers. With what timidity did Charlotte ask to see
Mr. George Smith, and with what puzzled amusement did
the receptionist convey the request to his employer? Two
simple maidens, he thought, but how extraordinarily froward
in asking to see the head of the firm! Or was it naïveté? Yet
there must have been something in Charlotte's eyes, in her
upright carriage and clear voice, that commanded instant
respect, for the attendant announced her to Mr. George
Smith without more ado. And so they came into the great
publisher's presence. He must have gazed at them in wonder.

ment—at the old-fashioned severity of toilet, at the dresses and bonnets that had certainly never been purchased at any Bond Street shop. Charlotte and Anne, as they stood quietly under his slightly austere scrutiny, were alien to anything he was accustomed to meet in the literary world. There was absolutely nothing about these two frail daughters of a Yorkshire clergyman, so out of their physical element in a London publisher's office, that would convey an inkling to Mr. George Smith of the creative fire he was playing with—unless perhaps it was a certain dignity and simple lack of pretension. He stood there, innocently unperceiving, on the brink of a startling discovery for which he was totally unprepared. Then Charlotte, with no word of explanation, handed him a letter. The dye was cast. George Smith glanced at the letter, and back at the open faces before him, for he recognized it as a letter he had written. And one quick, half-accusing, half-puzzled question slipped from George Smith's tongue: "Where did you get this?"

And Charlotte must have answered, "Why, you sent it to me!"

Mr. Smith's unspoken response to that one may well have been, "And who the devil are you?" but he undoubtedly restrained the impulse and replied with courteous doubt, "I did? And are *you* acting in behalf of Mr. Bell?"

When Charlotte made it clear who she was, and also the silent sister beside her, as well as the absent sister whom they could not persuade to leave the Haworth moors, and who together made the trinity of Bells, George Smith's ears must have vibrated with Olympian laughter! There was the letter in his hand, convincing evidence of the truth Charlotte had uttered. And George Smith rose magnificently to the occasion!

214

## Epilogue

THIS HAS not been (it was not meant to be) a book to fan the flames of controversy that still, and possibly will ever, burn like grass fire across the Haworth moors, in the attempt to "hole" some weary problem of truth or falsehood. True, there are several questions that haunt the biographers and critics of the fate-driven family of Brontës, as has been thoroughly illustrated by the many attempts to clarify their lives, but it has not been my purpose to re-examine the evidence pro and con.

The controversies I refer to include, among others, the question as to whether M. Heger encouraged Charlotte's infatuation, and even the question we ask ourselves: to what depths of passion did Charlotte herself descend? It would certainly appear, after reading the six letters that remain from those she wrote to M. Heger (possibly they were all she wrote), that *she* was sure she had been indelibly wounded, that her agony was mortal! Yet she did recover, as we know. And she not only survived this despair of the heart, but she was the one who eventually married. Furthermore, Charlotte was so fortunate as to live to see, as so few have ever done, literary fame reach heights undreamed of by any one of the sisters. Her four novels, even before her death, had achieved the reputation of being unique, even "classical." She was certainly one of the most important women of the mid-nineteenth century. That, in itself, must have been the greatest source of satisfaction and joy to a woman of Charlotte's nature, for she was, in so many ways, much more worldly and practical than Anne or Emily. Nor were the critics of her day mistaken. Her reputation has suffered little, if any, decline since her death. It might even be defended that she is constantly more assured of a place among the immortals. No one has left us, for instance, such a vivid portrayal of a moment in history: that industrialization of England, beginning as it did in the northern cities, and affecting as it did the country and the country people from Liverpool to Glasgow, and inaugurating a new era. And no one, until recent times, unless perhaps Arnold Bennett, has given us heroines of such living flesh and blood. Indeed, the women, the "little governesses," of Charlotte and Anne, are more realistic, withal so chaotic and romantic, than the women of such novelists as Dickens, Thackeray, Eliot, Meredith, Galsworthy. They are extraordinarily "modern" women. They have brains. They do things. They behave, to a startling degree, as if the single standard had already been invoked by the female sex.

I have not gone deeply into another question, also one of controversy, which throws doubt on the extent to which Branwell was involved with Mrs. Robinson. Branwell's own lurid accounts of his devotion and the lady's betrayals have many of the earmarks of pathological untruth, and it is quite possible that Mrs. Robinson has been much maligned.

Nor have I been too greatly concerned with a matter that is perhaps even more violent in its breech of opinion, the delineation of the character of Mr. Brontë. We have, on the one hand, those who paint this gentleman of the cloth with severest censure; who see him as cruel and cold, a man with no slightest flicker of human feeling, lacking the simplest understanding of his pathetic wife, Maria, and of his eight remarkable children; who starved them spiritually and physically; and who was to see them all die without visible suffering or remorse. While, again, we have some few biographers who, while admitting Patrick Brontë's severity and rigid religious discipline, yet believe that he could well have done worse by the glowing coals of genius he had inadvertently kindled; who point at the intellectual play of minds that early went on between father and daughters, at the remarkable library to which the children had access at all times (they were reading indiscriminately: the Bible, Shakespeare, Bunyan, Addison, Johnson, Sheridan, Cowper, Scott, Wordsworth, Coleridge, Byron, *Blackwood's Magazine*, and important London and provincial newspapers), and at the freedom allowed for the wing spread of imagination across the moors of Haworth; and who excuse the physical miseries, and the psychological blunders, as the ignorance of a man of Patrick Brontë's own upbringing, together with the religious bigotry of his day. Perhaps Patrick Brontë actually falls somewhere between these two extremes of portraiture. Certainly he was not loved by Emily and Charlotte as they grew older and were able to judge him. He spoiled and misunderstood his son, wrecking his life. And yet one cannot find it possible to be utterly harsh with Patrick Brontë. After all, he once lay in the sun and read *Paradise Lost*. Somewhere he, too, lost his Paradise. But he did something more for his children than merely conceive them. He gave them liberty, though it was, in the last analysis, "the liberty to die" that Emily Dickinson once asked for herself. A strange and awesome paradox!

Lastly, I have not attempted to dissect Emily, a task that has often led down confused and, it seems to me, futile paths

217

of failure. Emily was Emily, one of the most extraordinary and mysterious beings who ever lived; mysterious, and yet simplicity itself, as God is simple:

> The soul can split the sky in two
> And let the face of God shine through. *

Emily Brontë is the proof positive that what we call necessary experience pales to insignificance when placed in contrast to inner knowledge. She was a spirit that emerged independent of the material event. Perhaps no better description of her has been given than Maurice Maeterlinck's in *Wisdom and Destiny:*

> Not a single event ever paused as it passed by her threshold; yet did every event she could claim take place in her heart, with incomparable force and beauty, with matchless precision and detail. We say that nothing ever happened; but did not all things really happen to her much more directly and tangibly than with most of us, seeing that everything that took place about her, everything that she saw or heard, was transformed, within her thoughts and feelings, into indulgent love, admiration, adoration of life....
>
> Of her happiness, none can doubt. Not in the soul of the best of all those whose happiness has lasted longest, been the most active, diversified, perfect, could more imperishable harvest be found than in the soul Emily Brontë lays bare. If to her came nothing of all that passes in love, sorrow, passion, and anguish, still did she possess all that abides when emotion has faded away.

Emily's soul was forever innocent, forever completely knowing. Its beauty was beyond our words to touch. "And all

* "Renascence," by Edna St. Vincent Millay.

218

through" as May Sinclair has said, "an intangible presence, something mysterious, but omnipotently alive; something that excited these three sisters; something that atoned, but not only consoled for suffering and solitude and bereavement, but that drew its strength from these things; something that moved in their books like a soul; that they called 'genius.'"

Genius! It is the word that brings us back full circle to the spell of mystery and enchantment that caused me to write again (may my readers forgive me) the story of the "bewitched parsonage" of Haworth; back to the inexplicable flame, the wild chemistry of Celt and Cornish bloods, and, above all, the *furor scribendi* that seized these frail children and stretched them for a few shining seconds between the nodes of earth and sky.

# APPENDIX
## THE HEGER LETTERS *

### LETTER I

I am well aware that it is not my turn to write to you, but as Mrs. Wheelwright is going to Brussels and is kind enough to take charge of a letter—it appears to me that I ought not to neglect so favourable an opportunity of writing to you.

I am very pleased that the school-year is nearly over and that the holidays are approaching—I am pleased on your account, Monsieur—for I am told that you are working too hard and that your health has suffered somewhat in consequence. For that reason I refrain from uttering a single complaint for your long silence—I would rather remain six months without receiving news from you than add one grain to the weight, already too heavy, which overwhelms you. I know well that it is now the period of compositions, that it will soon be that of examinations and later on of prizes—and during all that time you are condemned to breathe the stifling atmosphere of the class-room—to spend yourself—to explain, to question, to talk all day, and then in the evening you have all those wretched compositions to read, to correct, almost to re-write—Ah, Monsieur! I once wrote you a letter that was less than reasonable; because sorrow was at my

* These letters were printed for the first time in the *London Times*, July 29, 1913. The caption above them reads: CHARLOTTE BRONTË'S "TRAGEDY." THE LOST LETTERS. DR. HEGER'S GIFT TO THE BRITISH NATION. TEXT AND TRANSLATIONS BY MARION H. SPIELMAN.

heart; but I shall do so no more.—I shall try to be selfish no longer; and even while I look upon your letters as one of the greatest felicities known to me I shall await the receipt of them in patience until it pleases you and suits you to send me any. Meanwhile I may well send you a little letter from time to time:—you have authorized me to do so.

I greatly fear that I shall forget French, for I am firmly convinced that I shall see you again some day—I know not how or when—but it must be for I wish it so much, and then I should not wish to remain dumb before you—it would be too sad to see you and not be able to speak to you. To avoid such a misfortune I learn every day by heart a half a page of French from a book written in a familiar style: and I take pleasure in learning this lesson, Monsieur; as I pronounce the French words it seems to me as if I were chatting with you.

I have just been offered a situation as first governess in a large school in Manchester, with a salary of £100 (i.e. 2,500 francs) per annum. I cannot accept it, for in accepting it I would have to leave my father, and that I cannot do. Nevertheless I have a plan—(when one lives retired the brain goes on working; there is the desire of occupation, the wish to embark on an active career). Our vicarage is rather a large house—with a few alterations there will be room for five or six boarders. If I could find this number of children of good family I should devote myself to their education. Emily does not care much for teaching but she would look after the housekeeping and although something of a recluse, she is too good hearted not to do all she could for the well-being of the children. Moreover she is very generous, and as for order, economy, strictness—and diligent work—all of them things very essential in a school—I willingly take that upon myself.

That, Monsieur, is my plan, which I have already explained to my father and which he approves. It only remains to find the pupils—rather a difficult thing—for we live rather far from towns and one does not greatly care about crossing the hills which form as it were a barrier around us. But the task that is without difficulty is almost without merit; there is great interest in triumphing over obstacles. I do not say I shall succeed— the effort alone will do me good. There is nothing I fear so much as idleness, the want of occupation, inactivity, the lethargy of the faculties: when the body is idle, the spirit suffers painfully.

I should not know this lethargy if I could write. Formerly I passed whole days and weeks and months in writing, not wholly without result, for Shelley and Coleridge—two of our best authors, to whom I sent certain manuscripts—were good enough to express their approval; but now my sight is too weak to write.—Were I to write much I should become blind. This weakness of sight is a terrible hindrance to me. Otherwise do you know what I should do, Monsieur?—I should write a book and I should dedicate it to my literature-master —to the only master I ever had—to you Monsieur. I have often told you in French how much I respect you—how much I am indebted to your goodness, to your advice; I should like to say it once in English. But that cannot be—it is not to be thought of. The career of letters is closed to me—only that of teaching is open. It does not offer the same attractions; never mind, I shall enter it and if I do not go far it will not be from want of industry. You too, Monsieur—you wished to be a barrister—destiny or Providence made you a professor; you are happy in spite of it.

Please convey to Madame the assurance of my esteem. I fear that Marie, Louise and Claire have already forgotten

223

me. Prospère and Victorine never knew me well; I remember well all five of them, especially Louise. She had so much character—so much naïveté in her little face.

Goodby, Monsieur.

Your grateful pupil

C. Bronte

July 24.

I have not begged you to write to me soon as I fear to importune you—but you are too kind to forget that I wish it all the same—yes, I wish it greatly. Enough; after all, do as you wish, Monsieur. If, then, I received a letter and if I thought that you had written it *out of pity*—I should feel deeply wounded.

It seems that Mrs. Wheelwright is going to Paris before going to Brussels—but she will post my letter at Boulogne. Once more goodbye, Monsieur; it hurts to say goodbye even in a letter. Oh, it is certain that I shall see you again one day— it must be so—for as soon as I shall have earned enough money to go to Brussels I shall go there—and I shall see you again if only for a moment.

LETTER II

[Addressed, on the back:—

Monsieur Heger

No. 32 Rue d'Isabelle

Bruxelles]

Monsieur,

I am in high glee this morning—and that has rarely happened to me these last two years. It is because a gentleman of my acquaintance is going to Brussels and has offered to take charge of a letter for you—which letter he will deliver to you himself, or else, his sister, so that I shall be certain that you have received it.

I am not going to write a long letter; in the first place, I have not the time—it must leave at once; and then, I am afraid of worrying you. I would only ask of you if you heard from me at the beginning of May and again in the month of August? For six months I have been awaiting a letter from Monsieur—six months' waiting is very long, you know! However, I do not complain and I shall be richly rewarded for a little sorrow if you will now write a letter and give it to this gentleman—or to his sister—who will hand it to me without fail.

I shall be satisfied with the letter however brief it be—only do not forget to tell me of your health, Monsieur, and how Madame and the children are, and the governesses and the pupils.

My father and my sister send you their respects. My father's infirmity increases little by little. Nevertheless he is not yet entirely blind. My sisters are well, but my poor brother is still ill.

Farewell, Monsieur; I am depending on soon having your news. The idea delights me for the remembrance of your kindnesses will never fade from my memory, and as long as that remembrance endures the respect with which it has inspired me will endure likewise.

Your very devoted pupil<br>C. Bronte

I have just had bound all the books you gave me when I was at Brussels. I take delight in contemplating them; they make quite a little library. To begin with, there are the complete works of Bernardin de St. Pierre—the Pensées de Pascal—a book of poetry, two German books—and (worth all the rest) two discourses of Monsieur le Professor Heger, delivered at the distribution of prizes of the Athenée Royal. Octb. 24th 1844

## LETTER III

[Addressed, on the back:—
Monsieur Heger
No. 32 Rue d'Isabelle
Bruxelles
Belgique]

Mr. Taylor has returned. I asked him if he had a letter for me. "No; nothing." "Patience," said I—"his sister will be here soon." Miss Taylor has returned. "I have nothing for you from Monsieur Heger," says she; "Neither letter nor message."

Having realized the meaning of these words, I said to myself what I should say to another similarly placed: "You must be resigned, and above all do not grieve at a misfortune which you have not deserved." I strove to restrain my tears, to utter no complaint.

But when one does not complain, when one seeks to dominate oneself with a tyrant's grip, the faculties start into rebellion and one pays for external calm with an internal struggle that is almost unbearable.

Day and night I find neither rest nor peace. If I sleep I am disturbed by tormenting dreams in which I see you always severe, always grave, always incensed against me.

Forgive me then, Monsieur, if I adopt the course of writing to you again. I cannot endure life if I made no effort to ease its sufferings.

I know that you will be irritated when you read this letter. You will say once more that I am hysterical (or neurotic)—that I have black thoughts, &c. So be it, Monsieur; I do not seek to justify myself; I submit to every sort of reproach. All I know is, that I cannot, that I will not, resign myself to lose wholly the friendship of my master. I would rather suffer the greatest physical pain than always have my heart lacerated by smarting regrets. If my master withdraws his friendship from me entirely I shall be altogether without hope; if he gives me a little—just a little—I shall be satisfied—happy; I shall have a reason for living, for working.

Monsieur, the poor have not need of much to sustain them —they ask only for the crumbs that fall from the rich man's table. Nor do I, either, need much affection from those I love. I should not know what to do with a friendship entire and complete—I am not used to it. But you showed me of yore a *little* interest, when I was your pupil in Brussels, and I hold on to the maintenance of that *little* interest—I hold on to it as I would hold on to life.

You will tell me perhaps—"I take not the slightest interest in you, Mademoiselle Charlotte. You are no longer an intimate of my House: I have forgotten you."

Well, Monsieur, tell me so frankly. It will be a shock to me. It matters not. It could be less dreadful than uncertainty.

I shall not reread this letter. I send it as I have written it. Nevertheless, I have a hidden consciousness that some people, cold and common-sense, in reading it would say— "She is talking nonsense." I would avenge myself on such persons in no other way than by wishing them one single day of the torment which I have suffered for eight months. We should then see if they would not talk nonsense too.

One suffers in silence so long as one has the strength so to do, and when that strength gives out one speaks without too carefully measuring one's words.

I wish Monsieur happiness and prosperity.

C. B.

Jany 8th Haworth. Bradford. Yorkshire.


## LETTER IV

Monsieur,

The six months of silence have run their course. It is now the 18th of Novr.; my last letter was dated (I think) the 18th of May. I may therefore write to you without failing in my promise.

The summer and autumn seemed very long to me; truth to tell, it has needed painful efforts on my part to bear hitherto the self-denial which I have imposed upon myself. You, Monsieur, you cannot conceive what it means; but suppose for a moment that one of your children was separated from you 160 leagues away, and that you had to remain six months without writing to him, without receiving news of him, without hearing him spoke of, without aught of his health, then you would understand easily all the harshness of such an obligation. I tell you frankly that I have tried meanwhile to forget you, for the remembrance of a person whom one thinks never to see again, and whom, nevertheless, one greatly esteems, frets too much the mind; and when one has suffered that kind of anxiety for a year or two, one is ready to do anything to find peace once more. I have done everything; I have sought occupations; I have denied myself absolutely the pleasure of speaking about you—even to Emily, but I have been able neither to conquer my regrets nor my impatience. That, indeed, is humiliating—to be unable to control

228

one's own thoughts, to be the slave of a regret, of a memory, the slave of a fixed and dominant idea which lords it over the mind. Why cannot I have just as much friendship for you, as you for me—neither more, nor less? Then should I be so tranquil, so free—I could keep silence then for ten years without an effort.

My father is well but his sight is almost gone. He can neither read nor write. Yet the doctors advise waiting a few months before attempting an operation. The winter will be a long night for him. He rarely complains; I admire his patience. If Providence wills the same calamity for me, may He at least vouchsafe me as much patience with which to bear it! It seems to me, Monsieur, that there is nothing more galling in great physical misfortunes than to be compelled to make all those about us share in our sufferings. The ills of the soul one can hide, but those which attack the body and destroy the faculties cannot be concealed. My father allows me now to read to him and write for him; he shows me too, more confidence than he has ever shown before, and that is a great consolation.

Monsieur, I have a favour to ask of you: when you reply to this letter, speak to me a little of yourself, not of me; for I know that if you speak of me it will be to scold me, and this time I would see your kindly side. Speak to me therefore of your children. Never was your brow severe when Louise and Claire and Prosper were by your side. Tell me also something of the School, of the pupils, of the Governesses. Are Mesdemoiselles Blanche, Sophie and Justine still at Brussels? Tell me where you travelled during the holidays—did you go to the Rhine? Did you visit Cologne or Coblentz? Tell me, in short, *mon maître*, what you will, but tell me something. To write to an ex-assistant-governess (No! I refuse to remember my employment as assistant-governess—I repudiate it)—anyhow, to write to an old pupil cannot be a very interesting occupation for you, I know; but for me it is life. Your last letter was stay and prop to me—nourishment to me, for half a year. Now I need another and you will give it me; not because you bear me friendship—you cannot have such—but because you are compassionate of soul and you would condemn no one to prolong suffering to save yourself a few moments' trouble. To forbid me to write to you, to refuse to answer me would be to tear from me my only joy on earth, to deprive me of my last privilege—a privilege I shall never consent willingly to surrender. Believe me, *mon maître,* in writing to me it is a good deed that you will do. So long as I believe you are pleased with me, so long as I have hope of receiving news from you, I can be at rest and not too sad. But when a prolonged and gloomy silence seems to threaten me with the estrangement of my master—when day by day I await a letter and when day by day disappointment comes to fling me back into overwhelming sorrow,—and the sweet delight of seeing your handwriting and reading your counsel escapes me as a vision that is vain, then fever claims me—I lose appetite and sleep—I pine away.

May I write to you again next May? I would rather wait a year, but it is impossible—it is too long.

C. Bronte

I must say a word to you in English—I wish I could write to you more cheerful letters, for when I read this over, I find it to be somewhat gloomy—but forgive me my dear master, do not be irritated at my sadness—according to the words of the Bible: "Out of the fulness of the heart, the mouth speaketh," and truly I find it difficult to be cheerful so long as I think I shall never see you more. You will perceive by the defects in this letter that I am forgetting the French language—I read all the French books I can get, and learn daily a portion by heart—but I have never heard French spoken but once since I left Brussels—and then it sounded like music in my ears—every word was most precious to me because it reminded me of you—I love French for your sake with all my heart and soul.

Farewell my dear master—may God protect you with special care and crown you with peculiar blessings.

C. B.

Novr. 18th Haworth. Bradford. Yorkshire.

NOTE: *It is on the edge of this letter that Professor Heger made some commonplace notes in pencil—one of them the name and address of a shoemaker.*

The Heger letters are reprinted through the courtesy of Hodder & Stoughton, Ltd., and the Bibliographical Society.

## EXTRACTS FROM REVIEWS

*Athenaeum,* no. 975, July 4, 1846, p. 682.
*Poems* by C. E. and A. Bell

The second book on our list furnishes another example of a family in whom appears to run an instinct of song. It is shared, however, by the three brothers—as we suppose them to be—in very unequal proportions; requiring in the case of Acton Bell the indulgences of affection . . . to make it music, —and rising, in that of Ellis into an inspiration, which may yet find an audience in the outer world. A fine quaint spirit has the latter, which may have things to speak that men will be glad to hear,—and an evident power of wing that may reach heights not here attempted. [Extracts follow from "The

231

Philosopher," "Song," and a poem beginning "Hope was but a timid friend."] The Muse of Currer Bell walks half way between the level of Acton's and the elevation attained by Ellis. It is rarely that the whole of one of his poems is up to the scale registered by parts. A bit here and there from the 'Monologue of the Teacher'... may give the tone and manner of his singing. [Extract follows.]

*Frasers Magazine*, Vol. 36, July-December, 1847, pp. 690-694.
Review of *Jane Eyre*

*Extract:*

... we wept over Jane Eyre. This, indeed, is a book after our own heart; and, if its merits have not forced it into notice by the time this paper comes before our readers, let us, in all earnestness, bid them lose not a day in sending for it. The writer is evidently a woman, and, unless we are deceived, new in the world of literature. But, man, or woman, young or old, be that as it may, no such book has gladdened our eyes for a long while. Almost all that we require in a novelist she has: perception of character, and power of delineating it; picturesqueness; passion; and knowledge of life.... The book closed, the enchantment continues... Reality—deep, significant reality—is the great characteristic of the book. It *is* an autobiography,—not, perhaps, in the naked facts and circumstances, but in the actual suffering and experience.... There are some defects in it.... There is, indeed, too much melodrama and improbability, which smack of the circulating library—we allude particularly to the mad wife and all that relates to her, and to the wanderings of Jane when she quits Thornfield.... Jane herself is a creation.... A creature of flesh and blood, with very fleshly infirmities, and very mortal excellencies; a woman, not a pattern.... Mr. Rochester is also well drawn, and from the life; but it is the portrait of a man drawn by a woman, and is not comparable to the portrait of Jane.

Extract from *The Times,* December 7, 1849,
*Shirley*—by the Author of *Jane Eyre*

... Struck, however, as we could not but be by the raciness and ability of the work [i.e., *Jane Eyre*], by the independent sway of a thoroughly original and unworn pen, by the masculine current of noble thoughts ... we perused the last words of the story with the conviction that the second effort of the author would not surpass the first.... Currer Bell, whomsoever that name may represent, during two-thirds of her performance [i.e., the first two volumes of *Jane Eyre*] obeyed the impulses and necessities of her mind, and her genius enabled her to command success; for the remaining third she was the mere bond slave of the booksellers.... Eager to extend renown, she starts from the point where she left off ... and presents us with ... a novel made up of third volumes [i.e., *Shirley*], a book to be read on the strength of the book that was formerly devoured.... *Shirley* is very clever as a matter of course. It could not be otherwise. The story of *Shirley* may be told in a couple of pages, yet a more artificial and unnatural history cannot be conceived; and what is true of the plot is even more applicable to the dramatis personae. The characters, from Shirley Keeldar down to the smallest boy in the narrative, are manufactured for the occasion.... *Shirley* is at once the most high-flown and the stalest of fictions.

# References

GRUNDY, FRANCIS H. *Pictures of the Past, Memories of Men I Have Met and Places I Have Seen.* London & Edinburgh, 1879.

LEYLAND, FRANCIS A. *The Brontë Family, with Special Reference to Patrick Branwell Brontë.* London: Hurst & Blackett, 1886. 2 vols.

BIRRELL, AUGUSTINE. *Life of Charlotte Brontë.* London: Walter Scott, 1887.

ROBINSON, A. MARY F. (Mme. James Darmesteter). *Emily Brontë.* London: Allen, 1889.

WRIGHT, DR. WILLIAM. *The Brontës in Ireland, or Facts Stranger than Fiction.* New York: D. Appleton & Co., 1893.

SHORTER, CLEMENT K. *Charlotte Brontë and Her Circle.* New York: Dodd, Mead & Co., 1896.

MACKAY, ANGUS, B. A. *The Brontës, Fact and Fiction.* London: Service & Paton, 1897.

MAETERLINCK, MAURICE. *Wisdom and Destiny.* Translated by Alfred Sutro. New York: Dodd, Mead & Co., 1898.

*Life and Works of the Sisters Brontë,* Haworth Edition. With Prefaces by Mrs. Humphrey Ward, and an Introduction and Notes to the Life, by Clement K. Shorter, 7 vols. New York and London: Harper & Brothers, 1899-1903.

235

BONNELL, HENRY H. *Charlotte Brontë, George Eliot, Jane Austen, Studies in Their Works.* New York: Longmans, Green & Co., 1902.

*Jane Eyre,* Introduction by May Sinclair, Everyman's Edition. New York: E. P. Dutton & Co., 1905.

SHORTER, CLEMENT K. *The Brontës, Life and Letters, Being an Attempt to Present a Full and Final Record of the Lives of the Three Sisters, Charlotte, Emily and Anne Brontë from the Biographies of Mrs. Gaskell and Others, and from Numerous Hitherto Unpublished Manuscripts and Letters.* New York: Charles Scribner's Sons, 1908.

MALHAM-DEMBLELY, JOHN. *The Key to the Brontë Works, Showing the Method of Their Construction and Their Relation to the Facts and People of Their Lives.* London & New York: The W. Scott Publishing Co., 1911.

SINCLAIR, MAY. *The Brontë Sisters,* with a Frontispiece (another edition titled *The Three Brontës*). London: Hutchinson & Co., 1912. Boston: Houghton Mifflin Co., 1913.

CHADWICK, ESTHER ALICE. *In the Footsteps of the Brontës.* London: Sir I. Pitman & Sons, 1914.

*Brontë Poems, Selections from the Poetry of Charlotte, Anne and Branwell Brontë,* Edited with an Introduction, by Arthur Christopher Benson, with Portraits and Facsimiles. New York and London: G. P. Putnam's Sons 1915.

SOUTHWART, ELIZABETH. *Brontë Moors and Villages from Thorton to Haworth,* with thirty-six illustrations by T. Mackenzie. London: John Lane, 1923. New York: Dodd, Mead & Co., 1923.

CROSS, WILBUR. *The Development of the English Novel.* New York and London: The Macmillan Co., 1923.

WOOLF, VIRGINIA. *The Common Reader* (essays on Charlotte and Emily Brontë). New York: Harcourt, Brace, 1925.

236

# REFERENCES

BRONTË, CHARLOTTE. *The Twelve Adventures, and Other Stories.* London: Hodder & Stoughton, Ltd., 1925.

DRINKWATER, JOHN. *A Book for Bookmen, Being Edited Manuscript and Marginalia with Essays on Several Occasions* (Essay on Patrick Branwell Brontë). New York: George H. Doran Co., 1927.

CLARKE, ISABEL C. *Haworth Parsonage, a Picture of the Brontë Family.* London: Hutchinson & Co., Ltd., 1927.

DIMNET, ERNEST. *The Brontë Sisters,* translated from the French, by Louise Morgan Sill. New York: Harcourt, Brace & Co., 1928.

WILSON, ROMER (Florence Roma Muir Wilson O'Brien). *The Life and Private History of Emily Jane Brontë,* with ten illustrations. New York: A. & C. Boni, 1928. London edition titled, *Alone, the Life and Private History of Emily Jane Brontë.* Chatto & Windus.

LANGBRIDGE, ROSAMUND. *Charlotte Brontë, a Psychological Study.* Garden City, N.Y.: Doubleday, Doran & Co., 1929.

ROMIEU, EMILIE and GEORGES. *The Three Virgins of Haworth, Being an Account of the Three Brontë Sisters,* translated from the French by Roberts Tapley. New York: E. P. Dutton & Co., 1930.

BENSON, E. F. *Charlotte Brontë.* London: Longmans, 1932.

MASSINGHAM, HUGH and A. J. (eds.). *The Great Victorians* (articles on Charlotte Brontë by Rebecca West, and on Emily Brontë by Charles Morgan). New York: Doubleday, Doran & Co., 1932.

RATCHFORD, FANNIE E., with the collaboration of William Clyde De Vane. *Legends of Angria, Compiled from the Early Writings of Charlotte Brontë.* New Haven: Yale University Press, 1933. London: H. Milford, Oxford University Press, 1933.

237

MOORE, VIRGINIA. *The Life and Eager Death of Emily Brontë, a Biography.* London: Rich & Cowan, Ltd., 1936.

KINSLEY, EDITH ELLSWORTH. *Pattern for Genius, a Story of Branwell Brontë and His Three Sisters Charlotte, Emily and Anne, Largely Told in Their Own Words.* New York: E. P. Dutton & Co., 1939.

RATCHFORD, FANNIE E. *The Brontës' Web of Childhood.* New York: Columbia University Press, 1941.

HATFIELD, C. W. (ed.). *The Complete Poems of Emily Brontë,* edited from the original manuscripts. New York: Columbia University Press, 1941.

KINKLEY, LAURA. *Ladies of Literature* (chapters on Charlotte and Emily Brontë). New York: Hastings House, 1946.

RAYMOND, ERNEST. *In the Steps of the Brontës.* London: Rich & Cowan, 1948.

*Five Essays Written in French by Emily Jane Brontë,* Now Translated by Lorine White Nagel with an Introduction and Notes, by Fannie E. Ratchford. Austin, Texas: University of Texas Press, 1948.

Brontë Society Transactions, Bradford, England, 1894—.